**SADLIER'S
Coming to Faith Program**
Catholic School Edition

Coming to God

Rev. Edward K. Braxton, Ph.D., S.T.D.
Dr. Elinor R. Ford
Eileen E. Anderson
Dr. Marie Murphy
Joseph F. Sweeney
Dr. Norman F. Josaitis
Gloria Hutchinson

with

Dr. Thomas H. Groome
Boston College

Scriptural Consultant
  Rev. Donald Senior, C.P., Ph.D., S.T.D.

Liturgical Consultant
  Sr. Catherine Dooley, O.P., Ph.D.

Pastoral Consultants
  Rev. Msgr. John F. Barry
  Rev. Virgil P. Elizondo, Ph.D., S.T.D.

Catechetical Consultants
  Sr. Maryanne Stevens, R.S.M., Ph.D.
  Gerard F. Baumbach
  Sr. Roseann Quinn, S.S.J.
  Sr. Diane Brooks, S.S.J.
  Sr. Carolyn Glynn, S.P.
  Sr. Jeannette Lucinio, S.P.
  Sr. Johanna Mullin, S.S.J.

Sadlier
A Division of
William H. Sadlier, Inc.
New York
Chicago
Los Angeles

Nihil Obstat
Reverend James J. Uppena
Censor Deputatus

Imprimatur
✠ Most Reverend Cletus F. O'Donnell
Bishop of Madison
December 16, 1987

The nihil obstat and imprimatur are official declarations that a book or pamphlet is free of doctrinal or moral error. No implication is contained therein that those who have granted the nihil obstat and imprimatur agree with the contents, opinions, or statements expressed.

Excerpts from the English translation of *The Roman Missal* © 1973, International Committee on English in the Liturgy, Inc. (ICEL). All rights reserved.

Copyright © 1988 by William H. Sadlier, Inc. All rights reserved. This book, or any part thereof, may not be reproduced in any form, or by any photographic, or mechanical, or by any sound recording system, or by any device for storage and retrieval of information, without the written permission of the publisher. Printed in the United States of America.

Home Office: 11 Park Place,
New York, NY 10007.
ISBN: 0-8215-1301-X
23456789/98

The photographs reproduced on the pages listed are from the following sources:

Berg & Associates 156 bottom.
Jim Bradshaw 87, 99 left.
Barbara Brockman 42.
Jim Carroll 40–41, 115, 117, 139, 163, 166, 172, 174, 175, 178, 179, 193, 194, 205, 223, 226, 250 left, 251 right, 252 top left, 252 bottom.
CLEO 68 top.
COMSTOCK 238, 239.
Jim Cronk 50 bottom, 79 right.
Michael DeFreitas 79 left, 196.
Joseph A. DiChello, Jr. 159.
Myrleen Ferguson 43 left, 44 left, 99 right, 149, 189, 241 top, 241 center.
Four by Five 34 left, 44–45 bottom, 45, 74–75 bottom.
FPG 206.
Ray Garcia 249.
David Grossman 119 top.
Robert Cushman Hayes 28, 29, 33, 48–49, 51 top, 58 right, 89 right, 94 top, 98, 102, 104, 118, 200 left, 207, 214.
Michal Heron 32, 50 top, 51 bottom, 69, 88, 201 right, 216–217, 237 top.
Susan Johns 236.
Leon V. Kofod 197.
Ed Kumler 61.
Lei 192, 204, 247 bottom, 248.
Freda Leinwand 49.
MacDonald Photo 54.
Mark IV 155.
Tom McGuire 89 left, 156 top.
Lawrence Migdale 136–137, 180.
Mark Mittleman 169, 176, 178, 181.
Monkmeyer: Bill Anderson 212 top; Bendick 212–213; Michal Heron 213.
Tom Myers 34 right, 237 bottom.
New England Stock Photo: Pris Petre 200.
Paul Robert Perry 38 bottom, 58 left.
Photo Edit 38 top, 120.
Picture Cube: Steve Weinrebe 250 right.
Positive Images: Jerry Howard 201 left.
Rainbow: Coco McCoy 241 bottom, Dan McCoy 58 bottom; Camilla Smith 148 bottom.
James L. Shaffer 154, 185, 187, 195, 247 top.
Nancy Sheehan 105, 219.
Victoria Beller Smith 21 right, 136 top.
J. Gerard Smith 246 top, 251.
THE STOCK SOLUTION: Royce Bair 39; Japan Create 44–45 top; Stephen Feld 97, 137, 216 top, 118 bottom; Michael Philip Manheim 108 top.
Erika Stone 119 bottom.
SYGMA: Giansanti 147.
Third Coast Stock Source: © 1982/ Eugene G. Shulz 21 left.
Wes Thomas 252 top right.
TOM STACK & ASSOCIATES: Jon Feingersh 68 bottom.
Mary Elenz Tranter 74 top, 108 bottom.
Unicorn: Bets Anderson Bailly 94 bottom, 215; Deneve Feigh Bunde 20; Martha McBride 43 right.
Jim Whitmer 63, 121–123, 125, 180, 196, 227, 229, 240, 246 top.
Bob Yellen 148 top, 184, 222.

Cover photo —
H. ARMSTRONG ROBERTS/M. Uselmann

Illustrations:
Creative Communicators Inc.
Irene Rofheart
Julie Landa
Nadina Simon

Cover art — Mari Goering

Dear Student,

Welcome to your first-grade religion book. This book is special because it will teach you all about Someone who has said to all of us,

"I have always loved you.
I will always love you."

That Someone is God.

This book was written especially for you.

Coming to God has many different activities to help you grow in your love for God and other people. These are:
- stories about boys and girls who love God just like you;
- special stories from the Bible;
- puzzles, games, and drawings to teach you about God;
- prayers to help you talk to and listen to God.

All of us hope that you will enjoy learning about God. We want you to come to love God more and more.

All of us in the Sadlier Family

Table of Contents

Letter to the Students   3

Unit I   God Gives Us the World

1. God Made the World	God made the world God made the animals God made everything Review Test Faith Alive at Home	8
2. God Made People	God made people God made you You are like God Review Test Faith Alive at Home	18
3. God Gives Us Life	God gives us life The gift of human life God's own life Review Test Faith Alive at Home	28
4. God Wants Us to Care	God knows and loves us We need people We must care for our world Review Test Faith Alive at Home	38
5. God's Promise	God's promise People turn away from God God keeps the promise Review Test Faith Alive at Home	48
6. The Bible	God's story The story of God's gifts The story of Jesus	58
7. All Saints	God's special friends Doing God's will The Feast of All Saints	62
8. Unit 1 Review		66
Unit 1 Test		67

Unit II God Gives Us Jesus

9.	The Story of Jesus	The birth of Jesus Jesus is human Jesus and our family Review Test Faith Alive at Home	68
10.	Jesus Is God's Son	Jesus is God's Son Jesus shows He is God Jesus shows God's love Review Test Faith Alive at Home	78
11.	Jesus Is Our Friend	Jesus cares for everyone Jesus heals the sick We pray to Jesus Review Test Faith Alive at Home	88
12.	Jesus Is Our Teacher	God our loving Parent The Law of Love God's love lasts forever Review Test Faith Alive at Home	98
13.	Jesus Gives Us Himself	The Last Supper Jesus dies and rises The Holy Spirit Review Test Faith Alive at Home	108
14.	Advent	God's promise Waiting for Jesus The birth of Jesus	118
15.	Christmas	The Christmas story Acting out the Christmas story Thanking God for Jesus	122
16.	Unit II Review		126
	Unit II Test		127
17.	First Semester Review		128
	First Semester Test		129

Unit III Jesus Christ Gives Us the Church

18.	The Holy Spirit	The Holy Spirit comes The Holy Spirit, the Helper The Holy Spirit and the Church Review Test Faith Alive at Home	130
19.	The Church Is for Everyone	Paul joins the Church You are part of the Church The Church is for everyone Review Test Faith Alive at Home	140
20.	The Church Celebrates Baptism	We celebrate Baptism Baptism makes us children of God We live like Jesus Review Test Faith Alive at Home	150
21.	The Church Celebrates (The Mass Begins)	Jesus gives us the Mass The Mass The Mass begins Review Test Faith Alive at Home	160
22.	The Church Celebrates (The Mass Continues)	Listening to God's Word Our gifts to God Holy Communion Review Test Faith Alive at Home	170
23.	Lent	Remembering Jesus' death The way of the cross Living like Jesus	180
24.	Easter	The story of Easter Acting out the story of Easter Thanking Jesus for new life	184
25.	Unit III Review		188
	Unit III Test		189

Unit IV Our Catholic Church and Us

26.	Our Parish Church	Our parish Helpers in our parish Belonging to the Catholic Church Review Test Faith Alive at Home	190
27.	Our Catholic Church	Catholics pray Celebrating the sacraments Being holy Review Test Faith Alive at Home	200
28.	The Church Helps People	Being fair Telling the Good News Being peacemakers Review Test Faith Alive at Home	210
29.	God Forgives Us	Being sorry God's forgiveness The Church forgives Review Test Faith Alive at Home	220
30.	God's Life Lasts Forever	With Jesus forever God's love lasts forever Jesus is with us always Review Test Faith Alive at Home	230
31.	A Prayer Service for Forgiveness	Readiness for Reconciliation	240
32.	Unit IV Review Unit IV Test		242 243
33.	Second Semester Review Second Semester Test		244 245
	Glossary		246
34.	My Mass Book My Prayer Book My Saints Book	 Saint Vincent de Paul Saint Thérèse of the Child Jesus Saint Nicholas	249 253 255

1 God Made the World

Our Life

Can you tell who made
    grasshoppers hop?
    frogs leap?
    ducks quack?

Can you tell who gave
    shape to the moon?
    light to the stars?
    fluff to the clouds?

Think about some things you know
about our wonderful world.
What are they?

God made everything good.

Sharing Life

Name something wonderful in our world. Tell someone why it is wonderful.

You Can Learn

- God made the world.
- God made the animals.
- God made everything good.

Our Faith

Who put the stars in the sky?
Who made sunshine?
Where did everything come from?

God Made the World

Everything belongs to God.
This is God's story!

God made the sun, the moon,
and the stars.
The light helps us see.
The light makes us warm.
God said, "It is good."
From Genesis 1:3–4

God made the water.
The water is good to drink.
The water makes plants grow.
God said, "It is good."
From Genesis 1:9

God made the earth.
God made the plants, trees,
and flowers.
God said, "It is good."
From Genesis 1:10–13

Name something that is good to drink.
Name something that smells good.
Thank God for making our world.

Who made the world?
How will you thank God for our world?

Our Faith (continued)

Who made the sun and the earth?
Who gave trunks to elephants?
Wings to birds?

God Made the Animals

God made all living things in our world.
God made so many wonderful animals!

Big animals were made by God.
Horses, lions, and elephants
were made by God!

Name some big animals.
Show how they move.

Little animals were made by God. Grasshoppers, kittens, and puppies were made by God!

Name some little animals. Show how they move.

The animals are God's gift to us. They are our helpers and friends. God wants us to be kind to animals.

Circle a big animal. Name it.

Circle a small animal. Name it.

Who made the animals? Thank God for the animals.

Our Faith (continued)

> Name your favorite animal.
> Who made it?
> Who made all the good things in our world?

God Made Everything

Creation is everything made by God.
All God's creation is good!
We know God through the things God made for us.

† Let us thank God for all these good things.

Thank You, God, for the sun and the moon and the stars.

Thank You, God, for mountains and oceans.

Thank You, God, for all creation.

Coming to Faith

Tell God's story of creation.
Color some things that God made.
Tell what you like best.
Tell why.

Faith Summary

- God is our Creator.
- God made everything.
- God made everything good.

Practicing Faith

Tell how you will thank God for making everything good.

When will you do it?

Color this thank-you prayer to God.
Do it with love.

Thank You, GOD, for Our Wonderful World.

Review Test

Read to me

Color the happy face to say "Yes."
Color the sad face to say "No."

1. God made everything good.

2. God's world is ugly.

3. God did not make the animals.

4. God is our creator.

5. I will say thank you to God for all creation.

Faith Alive at Home

Reading the *Faith Summary* on page 15 will help your family learn what was taught this week. Here are some things you may do to help your children know and live their faith.

Creation prayer
This week, your child learned that God is our Creator. Pray together the thank-you prayer he or she colored. Ask your child what she or he was thankful for and why.

Creation posters
Have fun with your child by finding and cutting out magazine and newspaper pictures of animals and things in God's creation. Help him or her to paste the pictures on a large sheet of paper to be kept in your child's room.

2 God Made People

Our Life

What do you like to do? Mark the things you like to do best.

Name some other things you can do.

You belong to God.
You are wonderful.

Sharing Life

How do you feel when you do these things? Tell about it.

Why can you do all these things?

You Can Learn

- God made people.
- God made you wonderful.
- You are to be like God.

Our Faith

Show some things you can do.
Why can you do so many things?
Tell a friend your answer.

God Made People

Everything God made is good.
God made people.
People are very special.

Read to me from the Bible

God said, "Let Us make people.
They will be like Us."
So God made people.
God made a man and a woman.
God said, "People are very good."
From Genesis 1:26–31

God made all kinds of people.
God made big people
and small people.

God made people with dark skin.
God made people with light skin.
No two people are exactly alike.

All people are beautiful
because God made us all.
We are all God's children.
God loves us all.
We are to love one another.

† Thank You, God, for all kinds
of people.

Who made people?
Why are people so special?

Our Faith (continued)

Why are people special?
What special things can you do?

God Made You

Before you were born,
God called you by name.
God said, "What a wonderful person
_____ Kolbe _____ will be!"
God gave you
your eyes for seeing,
your ears for hearing,
your nose for smelling,
your mouth for talking and tasting,
and your hands for feeling
and holding, and hugging.
How wonderfully made you are!

God made you.
God loves you.
God loves every part of you.

I can see.

I can touch.

I can hear.

Faith Word
Create means to make something new.

Color and pray
† God, You created me.
# I AM
wonderfully made.
From Psalm 139

I can taste.

I can smell.

Who made you so wonderful?
What wonderful things can you do?
How will you thank God for making you so wonderful?

23

Our Faith (continued)

What wonderful things can you do?
Why are you so special?

You Are Like God

God knows, and loves, and creates.
God made you to know, and love,
and create.

A teddy bear is a wonderful thing.
But a teddy bear cannot know things.
You can know many things.
God made you to know and learn.

A teddy bear is a wonderful thing.
But a teddy bear cannot love.
A teddy bear cannot give you a hug.
You can hug. You can love.
God made you to love everyone.

A teddy bear is a wonderful thing.
But a teddy bear cannot draw
a picture.
You can draw. You can make music.
You can create something new.

You can know, and love, and create.
You are to be like God.

Coming to Faith

Match the pictures with the words that show how you are like God.

know　　　　　love　　　　　create

Do you believe that God made you wonderful?
How does that make you feel?

Faith Summary
- God made people.
- God made you wonderful.
- You are to be like God.
- You can know, love, and create things.

Practicing Faith

Here are some things you can do that show you are like God.

Draw yourself in these pictures.

I want to know.

I will love.

I will create.

Which of these will you do?
When will you do them?
How will you thank God
for making you so wonderful?

Review Test

Read to me

Color the happy face to say "Yes."
Color the sad face to say "No."

1. God loves you.

2. A teddy bear can know things.

3. God made people.

4. A teddy bear can create things.

5. I am happy God loves me.

Faith Alive at Home

Reading the *Faith Summary* on page 25 will help your family learn what was taught this week. Here are some things you may do to help your family know and live its faith.

Family photo album
Look with your child through your family photo album or at other pictures of friends. Show your child some of the people who are part of the family's life. Talk about the different things they do.

Say a prayer
You and your child might like to say this prayer:

† Thank You, God, for making people.
Thank You, God, for making me so wonderful.
Thank You, God, for making me like You.

27

3 God Gives Us Life

Our Life

How would you feel
if nothing made sounds?

What sounds do
      lions make?
      puppies make?
      children make?
Can you make these sounds? Do it.

How would you feel
if nothing moved?

How do
      dolphins move?
      birds move?
      children move?
Can you make these movements?
Do it.

Life is a wonderful gift.

Sharing Life

Can a rock make sounds?
Can a rock move?

What can you do that a rock cannot do? Why?

What do you like best about being alive?

You Can Learn

- God gives us the gift of life.
- God gives us the gift of human life.
- God gives us God's own life.

Our Faith

How is a rock different from a puppy?
Name some other things that are alive.

God Gives Us Life

When God made the world, God made living things, too. The Bible story tells us what God told all living things to do.

Read to me from the Bible

God told all the fish in the water to fill the sea, all the birds in the air to fill the sky, and all the animals on the land to fill the earth.

From Genesis 1:20–24

What a wonderful gift life is.
Imagine all that living things can do.

Living things can move.
Living things can fly.
There are living things that grow.
There are living things that crawl,
and walk, and make sounds.

There are living things
all over the world.
Living things are gifts from God.

† Thank You, God,
for all living things.

Who gives the gift of life?
How will you thank God today
for the gift of life?

Our Faith (continued)

Who made all living things?
What is good about being alive?

The Gift of Human Life

Of all the things God made,
God loves people most.
People are more important
than plants and animals.
People have human life.

Human life is our gift from God.
Human life is always special.
Human life is very precious to God.
God gives us the gift of human life
through our parents.

Why is human life always special?

Faith Word
Human life is our gift of life from God.

God wants us to care for all living things.
God wants us to care especially
for human life.

Who cares for you?
Is there someone you help care for?

How are people different from
plants and animals?

Pray alone
✝ Thank You, God, for the gift of life.

Draw
a picture of yourself caring for a living thing.

Who gives us the gift of human life?
Show how you feel about being alive.

33

Our Faith (continued)

What do you like best about being alive?
Who gives you the gift of life?

God's Own Life

God is our loving Parent.
We are God's children.
God gives us God's own life.
We call God's life in us grace.

Grace is a special gift.
It is God's own life and love.
You have God's grace.
You can say,
"God is my loving Parent.
I am God's own child."

Who gives us God's own life?
How does this make you feel?

Review Test

Read to me

Color the happy face to say "Yes."
Color the sad face to say "No."

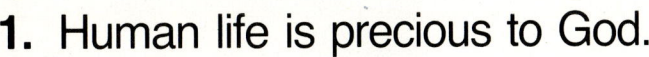

1. Human life is precious to God.

2. God's life in us is called grace.

3. A rock can hop.

4. I have the gift of human life.

5. I am happy to be God's child.

Faith Alive at Home

Reading the *Faith Summary* on page 35 will help your family learn what was taught this week. Here are some things you may do to help your family know and live its faith.

Thank God for life
Recall for your child the story of his or her birth or adoption. Share with your child how wonderful it is to watch him or her grow.

Say a prayer
You might like to pray together with your child. Thank God for the gift of your child's life. You may wish to say:

† Thank You, God, for the gift of ____(child's name)____ life. Please help him or her to grow in Your love.

37

4 God Wants Us to Care

Our Life

Do these people know one another?
How can you tell if someone knows you?
Who knows you?
Whom do you know?

Do these people love one another?
How can you tell if someone loves you?
Who loves you?
Whom do you love?

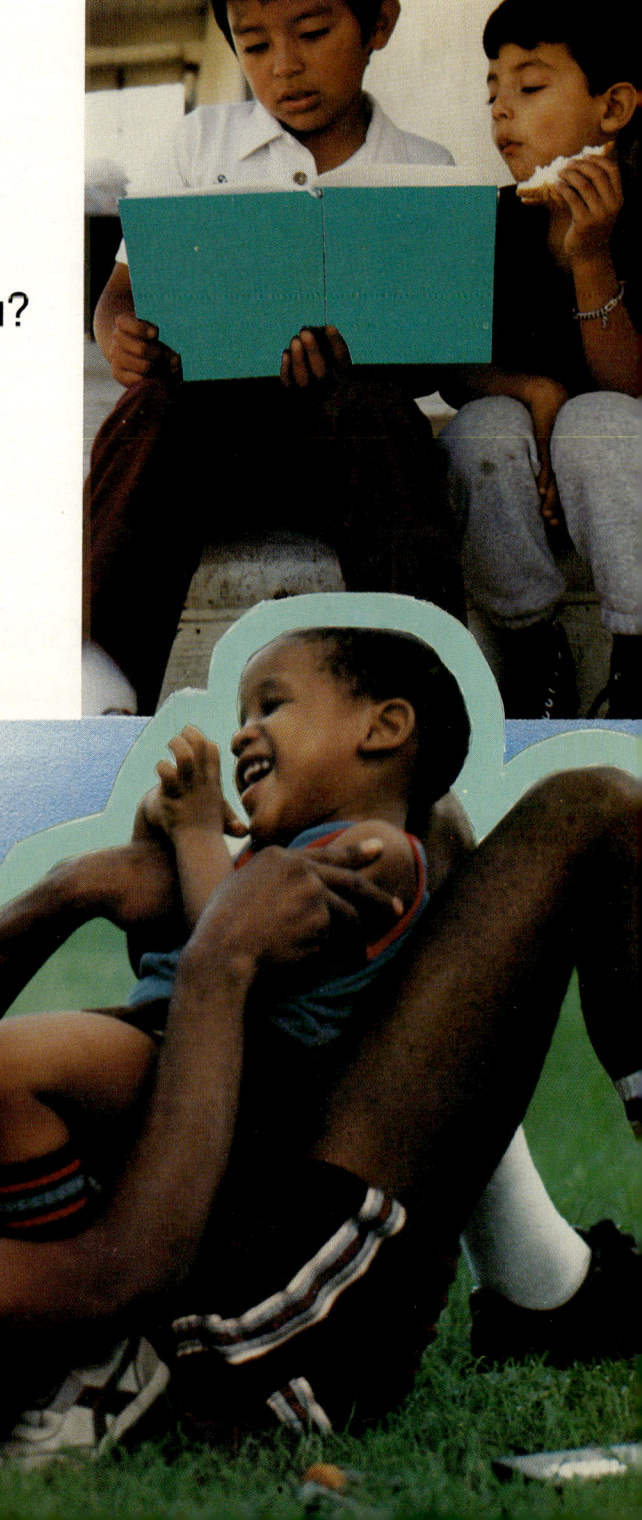

God knows and loves us.

Sharing Life

Who helps you know other people?
Who helps you love others?
Do you think God wants us to love one another?

You Can Learn

- God knows and loves us.
- People need other people.
- God made us to care for the world.

Our Faith

Tell something about your family.
Tell something you know about God.

God Knows and Loves Us

There is only one God.
There are three Persons
in our one God.
The three Persons in God are
God the Father,
God the Son,
and God the Holy Spirit.

We call the three Persons
in one God the Blessed Trinity.

The three Persons in God
are like a family.
They know one another.
They love one another forever.

The three Persons in God
know and love us.
How wonderful it is that God
knows and loves us.
We know and love God, too.

When we begin our prayers to God, we say,
✝ In the name of the Father,
and of the Son,
and of the Holy Spirit.
We call this the
Sign of the Cross.

Make the Sign of the Cross now.
Will you say this prayer before you go to bed tonight?

Our Faith (continued)

How do we begin our prayers?
Why do we need other people?

We Need People

Think of how many people there are.
There are people near us.
There are people far away.
There are people all over the world.

People need other people.
We were made for one another.
A goldfish can live alone in a bowl.
A canary is happy by itself.
But God made people to be friends.

God wants us to care
for one another.

We care for people when
they are sad
or when they are lonely.
We care for people
when they are afraid.
We care for one another
when we are happy.

How good it is to laugh
with a friend,
or to make someone glad.

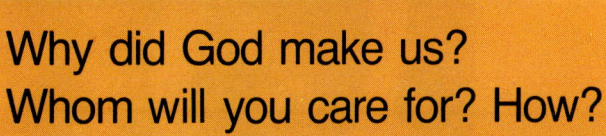

Why did God make us?
Whom will you care for? How?

Our Faith (continued)

How do you care for people?
How can you care for our world?

Our Beautiful World

We are part of the wonderful world
God made.
God gives us our beautiful world.
God wants us to take care of
and enjoy our world.

We plant seeds.
We sail on the sea.
We can fly through space.

Each of us can do something
to keep our world beautiful.
Name one thing that you care for in
the world. Tell how you care for it.

Coming to Faith

Draw something you can help care for.

Why does God want us to love one another?
Why does God want us to care for the world?

Faith Summary

- God knows us and loves us.
- God made us to know and love one another.
- God made us to care for the world.

45

Practicing Faith

God made us
to care for one another.
We need other people.

Draw or paste a picture here
of someone whom you can help.

When will you do it?

Faith Alive at Home

Reading the *Faith Summary* on page 45 will help your family learn what was taught this week. Here are some things you may do to help your children know and live their faith.

Talk about caring
Have your child show you the pictures of people caring for each other. Ask how he or she thinks they are caring for people. Talk with your child about the picture of him or her caring for something.

Review Test

Read to me

Color the happy face to say "Yes."
Color the sad face to say "No."

1. God does not know me.

2. God the Son is part of the Blessed Trinity.

3. People need other people.

4. God made us to care for the world.

5. Draw how you will care for our world.

Say a prayer
Pray together with your child about caring for God's creation. You may wish to say the following:

† Help us, God, to care for one another.
Help us to care for our world.

5 God's Promise

Our Life

Read to me

A promise is a special thing
I say that I will do.
The reason that it's special is
I give my word to you.

I promise I will be your friend
in good times or in bad.
I promise to be with you when
you're happy or you're sad.

A promise can be broken, but
I hope that mine won't be.
I want to be the kind of friend
who keeps his word, you see.

Who are your friends?
Do you make promises to them?
Do you ever break your promises
to them?

We are never alone.

Sharing Life

How do you feel when someone promises to be your friend?

How would you feel if someone broke a promise to be your friend?

Why do we sometimes break our promises?
Why should we keep our promises?

You Can Learn

- God promises to be with us always.
- People turn away from God.
- God keeps the promise to love us always.

Our Faith

What is a promise?
What does this mean,
 "I promise I will always
 be your friend"?

God Makes a Promise

God promises to be with us always. Here is a story of the home God made for the first man and woman. Their names were Adam and Eve.

Read to me from the Bible

In the beginning God planted a beautiful garden. God put the man and the woman in the garden. They were to be happy there always. They were to do what God asked. God asked them not to eat the fruit of one special tree.

From Genesis 2:8–25

God asked Adam and Eve to choose. They could love or not love God. God wanted them to choose what was right.

God wants us to choose
what is right.
God wants us to live
as God's children.
We can love or not love God.

We can love
or not love one another.

What does God promise us?
What will you promise God?

Our Faith (continued)

How do you show you are God's child? Did you ever do something you should not have done? How did you feel?

People Turn from God

God gave Adam and Eve
a beautiful home.
They had all they needed.
They would be happy
with God forever.

Read to me from the Bible

The Bible story tells us that Adam and Eve turned away from God. They did what God asked them not to do. Then they hid from God. What do you think God did? God came looking for them. God never stopped loving them.

From Genesis 3:6–9

Sometimes we do what we should not do.
But God never stops loving us,
no matter what we do.
God loves and cares for us always.
We can be happy with God forever.

◀ **Write**
one word to tell how you feel
because God loves you.

_____

- -

_____

Can you thank God for
always loving you? How?
Will you thank God?

Our Faith (continued)

Who promises to love you always?
How can you show you love God?

God Keeps the Promise

When Adam and Eve said no to God,
they were sad and lonely.
But God did not leave them alone.
God promised to be with them always.

God kept God's promise.
God gave us Jesus, God's own Son.
Jesus shows us how to love God.

Jesus shows us how to love
one another.
If we live as Jesus shows us, we
can be happy with God forever.

† Thank You, God, for keeping
Your promise.

Coming to Faith

What does God promise us? Color these words to help you remember God's promise.

What does that tell you about God? What does that tell you about yourself?

I Will

Love You

Always

Faith Summary
- God promises to be with us always.
- People turned away from God.
- God keeps God's promise.
- God gives us Jesus, God's own Son.

Practicing Faith

God made a promise
to love us always.
Can you make a promise to God?

Can you say,
✝ "I always want to be with You,
God"?

If you want to say "Yes," color this rainbow.

How will you show other people
that you are God's own child?
When will you do it?

Faith Alive at Home

Reading the *Faith Summary* on page 55 will help your family learn what was taught this week. Here are some things you may do to help your children know and live their faith.

Write a promise
Ask your child to tell you about the promise he or she made and colored in class. Say this, as a prayer with your child. Then write your own promise. For example, "I, too, want to be with You, God." Show it to your child.

Review Test

Read to me

Color the happy face to say "Yes."
Color the sad face to say "No."

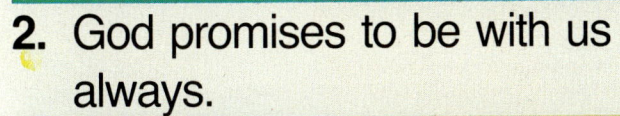

1. Adam and Eve turned away from God.
2. God promises to be with us always.
3. God never stops loving us.
4. God keeps God's promise.
5. Show how you would feel if someone broke a promise. Use the circle for a face.

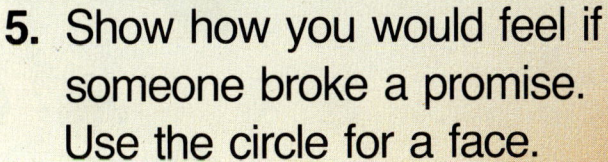

Keeping promises
You might like to spend some time explaining to your child that at times it is impossible to keep promises.

6 The Bible

Our Life

Do you have a favorite book? Tell about it.

Sharing Life

Imagine that your class is going to write a book about God. What would you want to say in the book?

58

Our Faith

A long time ago some people wanted to tell God's story. They thought about who made the world. They thought about who made them.

God helped the people to find the answers. They wrote the story of all that God had done for them. We call God's story the Bible.

The stories in the Bible tell us about God and God's gifts to us. What do you know about God? Name some of God's gifts to us.

The Bible tells us about God's best gift. God's best gift is Jesus Christ, God's own Son.

Coming to Faith

Tell a friend why the Bible is a special book.

What stories from the Bible do you know?

Draw a picture of your favorite Bible story. Talk about your picture with a friend.

Faith Alive at Home

If possible, place a child's version of the Bible in a special place in your home. Reserve some time to invite your child to tell you about his or her favorite Bible story. Then read that story from your child's Bible.

Practicing Faith

Help make a beautiful place for the Bible in your classroom.

Teacher: Let us walk in procession and place the book that tells God's story, the Bible, in a special place.

† **Bible Prayer Service**

Leader: God helped people to write God's story.

All: Thank you, God.

Leader: The Bible tells us about God's people and, most of all, about Jesus.

All: Thank you, God.

Leader: The Bible tells us about God's gifts to us.

All: Thank you, God.

Leader: We have learned about the Bible, God's story. The Bible can help us to love God and other people.

7 All Saints

Our Life

Name some of the special people in your life.
Draw a picture of one of these special people.

Share your picture with a friend.

Sharing Life

Imagine you can spend one day doing anything you want for your special friend.
What would you do?

Tell the class about your idea.

Our Faith

In our Church we celebrate some special people each year on November 1. These special people are called saints.

Saints are people who loved God very much. They did God's will during their life on earth. Now they are happy with God forever in heaven.

When they were alive, the saints tried to do all the things Jesus told us to do.

They:
>fed the hungry,
>gave clothes to poor people,
>prayed each day,
>shared their things with others,
>were kind and fair to everyone.

We do not know the names of all the saints who are with God in heaven. The Church celebrates the feast of All Saints to remember and honor all of them.

Coming to Faith

An All Saints Play

Leader: The saints are people who will live with God forever in heaven. Anyone can become a saint. Today we will meet some special people who became saints.

Saint Elizabeth: I gave food to people who were poor and hungry.

Saint Peter: I followed Jesus wherever He went. When He died, I told people about Jesus.

Saint Thérèse: I prayed for people to help them get to know Jesus.

Saint Joseph: I was Jesus' foster father. I cared for Jesus and Mary.

Leader: There are many more people who are saints. Can anyone tell something about another saint?

Saint Elizabeth

Saint Joseph

Practicing Faith

☦ All Saints Celebration

Leader: Let us ask the saints to help us live as friends of Jesus. Saint Elizabeth,

All: Pray for us.

Leader: Saint Peter,

All: Pray for us.

Leader: Saint Thérèse,

All: Pray for us.

Leader: Saint Joseph,

All: Pray for us.

Leader: May all the saints in heaven pray for us, that we may live as friends of Jesus.

Faith Alive at Home

Tell your child about a saint to whom you give special devotion.

8 Unit I Review

Creation is everything made by God.

God made the world and all things in it.
Everything God made is good.
People are especially important to God.
God wants people to care for all living things.

God gives you God's own life.

Grace is God's own life and love in you. You can say, "God is my loving Parent. I am God's own child."

God knows and loves us.

There is only one God.
There are three Persons in God: God the Father, God the Son, and God the Holy Spirit.
The three Persons in God know and love us.

God loves and cares for us always.

Sometimes we do what is wrong. Even then, God loves and cares for us always.
God gives us Jesus, God's own Son, to show us how to love God and one another.

Unit I Test

Read to me

Color the happy face to say "Yes."
Color the sad face to say "No."

1. Everything God made is good.

2. I am God's own child.

3. The three Persons in one God know and love us.

4. Sometimes God does not love us.

5. Draw a picture of something you love that God gave you.

67

9 The Story of Jesus

Our Life

Read to me

"We have such a beautiful baby," Mrs. Howard said.

She handed the tiny baby to her husband and stepped into the car.

The child had been born in Saint Luke's Hospital a few days before. The proud parents were taking their new baby home for the first time.

What is special about babies?
What do you know about the day you were born?
How can you show that you are happy to be alive?

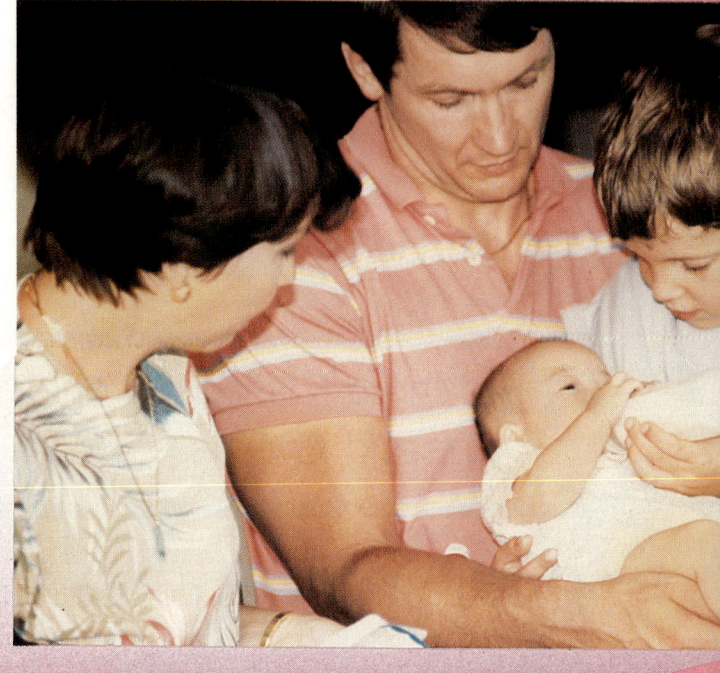

We are a family.

Sharing Life

Have you ever seen or hugged a new baby?
How did you feel?
Why are people happy when a baby is born? Tell about it.

You Can Learn
- Jesus is born.
- Jesus is one of us.
- Jesus is part of our human family.

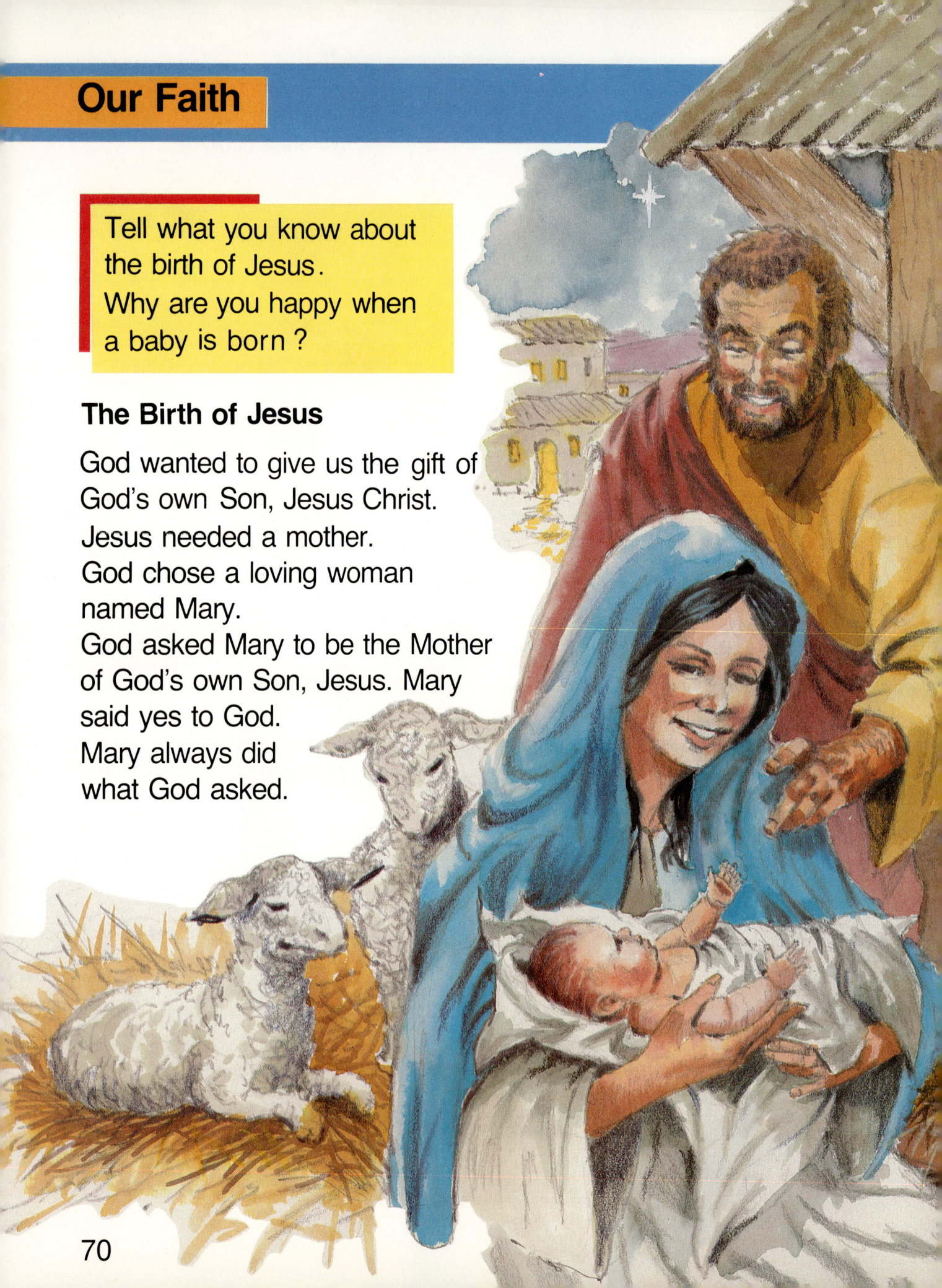

Our Faith

> Tell what you know about the birth of Jesus.
> Why are you happy when a baby is born?

The Birth of Jesus

God wanted to give us the gift of God's own Son, Jesus Christ.
Jesus needed a mother.
God chose a loving woman named Mary.
God asked Mary to be the Mother of God's own Son, Jesus. Mary said yes to God.
Mary always did what God asked.

Faith Word
Christmas is when we celebrate the birth of Jesus.

Read to me from the Bible

Mary was married to Joseph. They went to a town called Bethlehem. There was no room for them at the inn. So they had to stay in a stable. There Mary gave birth to Jesus, God's own Son. Mary laid Jesus in a manger.
From Luke 1:26–38

We celebrate Jesus' birth at Christmas.

◀ **Act out**
the Christmas story with your friends.

What is the best gift God gives us?
How will you thank God for Jesus?

71

Our Faith (continued)

Who is Jesus?
Do you think Jesus was like you? How?

Jesus Is Human

Do you think Jesus laughed, and played, and sang? Do you think Jesus ever felt afraid or alone? Do you think Jesus got tired?

Think of the things you love to do. Jesus did some of them, too. He laughed and played with His friends.

He loved and cared for them. At times Jesus was sad or tired, too.
Jesus is one of us.

Jesus learned how to read and write. He studied the Holy Bible. He learned from Mary and Joseph how to love and pray and work.

Jesus, Mary, and Joseph did the things that families do together.

Imagine being with Jesus, Mary, and Joseph.
How does that make you feel?

◀ **Color**
the Holy Family at home.

How is Jesus like us?
What do you like best about the Holy Family?
How will you help your family to be holy?

Our Faith (continued)

What did Jesus do with His family?
How do you help your family?

Jesus and Our Family

There are many kinds of families.
Some are big, others are small.
Some have two parents, and others have one.
Some families live together, others do not.
Which kind of family do you have?

People who belong to families love one another.
They want the best for one another.
Jesus wants the best for us, too.
Jesus is part of your family and every family that believes in Him.

Who belongs to Jesus' family?

Coming to Faith

Connect the dots.
Decorate the banner.

Jesus is part of my

family

How do you feel about having Jesus as part of our human family?

Faith Summary

- Jesus is God's own Son.
- Jesus is one of us.
- Jesus is part of our human family.

Practicing Faith

How will you show you are happy that Jesus is part of your family? What will you do?

Draw yourself in the picture showing how you will help at home. When will you do it?

Faith Alive at Home

Reading the *Faith Summary* on page 75 will help your family to learn what was taught this week. Here are some things you may do to help your children know and live their faith.

Think of a time when Jesus was happy, or sad, or tired. Tell your child about it.

Looking at pictures
Admire your child's drawing on this page. Then take a few minutes to talk about other ways your child can help at home.

Review Test

Read to me

Write the missing word on each line.

Christmas   Jesus   Mary

1. ____ was born in Bethlehem.

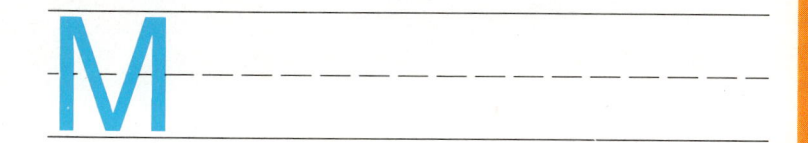

   J_____

2. We celebrate Jesus' birth at ____ .

   C_____

3. God chose ____ to be Jesus' Mother.

   M_____

4. Imagine that you are playing with Jesus.
   Draw a picture of Jesus and you.

Praying to Jesus
Remind your child that Jesus is part of our human family. Say this prayer with your child.

† Dear Jesus, thank You for loving me.
Thank You for loving my family.
Thank You, Jesus, for loving everyone.
We all love You, too.

10 Jesus Is God's Son

Our Life

I like games.
I like toys.
I like gifts for girls and boys.

You like games.
You like toys.
Do your gifts all bring you joys?

What gift would you like to receive?
What gift would you like to give?
Who is going to receive your gift?
How do gifts make you feel?

Jesus is God's greatest gift to us.

Sharing Life

Some gifts come in boxes.
Some do not.

Can you put a hug in a box?
Can a hug be a gift? Why?

Can you put a friend in a box?
Can a friend be a gift? Why?

Can love be a gift? Why?
How can you give someone love?

Act out a way you can give love.
Why is love the best gift of all?

You Can Learn
- Jesus is God's own Son.
- Jesus shows us He is God's Son.
- Jesus shows us God loves us.

Our Faith

What kind of gift does not come in a box?
What gift is the best of all?

Jesus Is God's Son

God gives us many gifts.
God's greatest gift to us is
God's Son, Jesus.

Read to me from the Bible

One day when Jesus was grown,
He saw His cousin John.
John told people to get ready.
He said Someone Special was coming.
One day, John baptized Jesus in the
River Jordan. God said to Jesus,
"You are My own dear Son.
I am pleased with You."
From Mark 1:9–1

Jesus traveled from place to place with His friends. He told people about God. He helped people who needed Him.

Jesus showed the people how much God loved them. He showed them how to love and care for one another.

Jesus showed, by what He did and said, that He was God's own Son.

Why is Jesus God's greatest gift to us? When will you thank God for giving us Jesus?

Our Faith (continued)

Tell some ways that Jesus showed He was God's Son. What did Jesus teach the people?

Jesus Is God

Jesus showed people how to love God.
Jesus showed them how to love one another.
Jesus did things only God could do.

Read to me from the Bible

One day, Jesus and His friends were in a boat.
It began to rain. The wind blew.
The waves rocked the boat.
Jesus' friends were afraid.
Jesus stood up and said to the sea, "Be quiet!"

The rain and the wind stopped.
The sea was quiet.
The friends of Jesus said,
"Who can this be that the wind
and the sea obey Him?"
From Mark 4:35–41

Jesus' friends knew that only God could stop a storm at sea.

◀ **Write**
Jesus is

God's own Son.

How did people know that Jesus was the Son of God? What will you do to show Jesus you love Him?

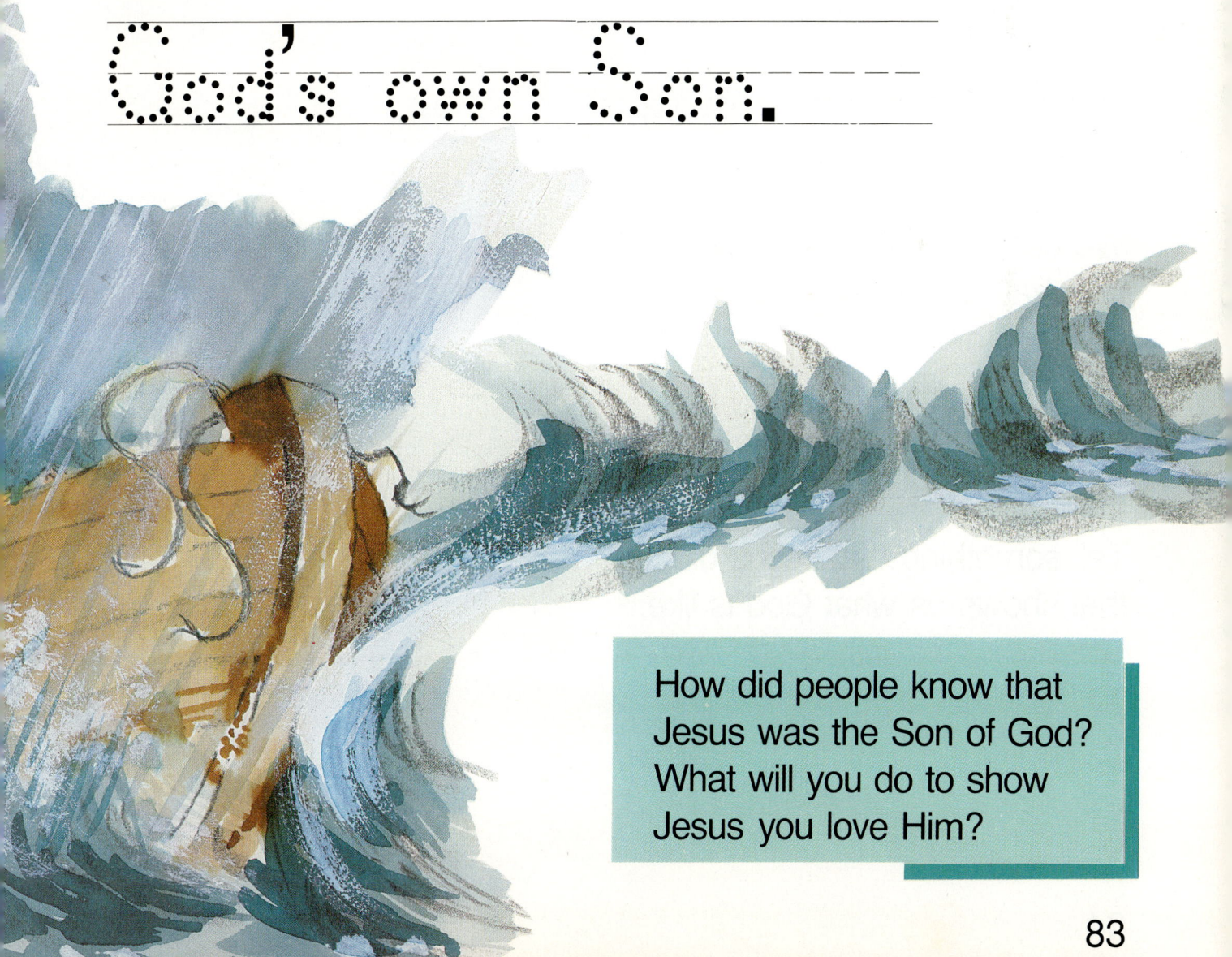

Our Faith (continued)

Who is Jesus?
What do you know about Jesus?

Jesus Shows Us God

Jesus is one of us, and Jesus is God.
People could see Jesus.
They could touch Him,
and hear Him,
and look at His face.

People may ask us,
"What is God like?"
We can say that Jesus showed us what God is like by what He said and did.

Jesus said, "Anyone who has seen Me has seen the Father."

From John 14:9

Tell something that Jesus did that shows us what God is like.

Coming to Faith

Find the missing word.
Color all the spaces with an X.
Print the word in these sentences.

Jesus is the Son of ____ .

_____

Jesus shows us what ____ is like.

_____

How do you know that God loves you?
What does Jesus show you about God?

Faith Summary

- Jesus is God's greatest gift to us.
- Jesus is God's own Son.
- Jesus shows us He is God.
- Jesus shows us God's love.

85

Practicing Faith

Color this picture of Jesus.

Show it to someone.
Tell them that Jesus is
God's best gift.

What will you do to show Jesus you love Him?

What will you do today to thank God for the gift of Jesus?

Faith Alive at Home

Reading the *Faith Summary* on page 85 will help your family to learn what was taught this week. Here are some things you may do to help your children know and live their faith.

† **Prayer of thanks**
Read this passage to your child:
"God so loved the world that God sent God's own Son into the world."
From John 3:16

Pray in your own words, thanking God for the gift of Jesus.

Review Test

Read to me

Write the missing word on each line.

        love   Jesus   Son

1. Jesus is God's own ____ .

S _____

2. Jesus shows us God's ____ .

l _____

3. ____ shows us what God is like.

J _____

4. Circle what you will do today.

      pray to Jesus   be mean   help a friend

Sharing
Have your child show you the picture he or she colored. Share with him or her some of your own personal thoughts about Jesus. Let your child share his or her thoughts with you.

11 Jesus Is Our Friend

Our Life

Read to me

I want to draw a picture of
The best friend there could be.
Here's what I'll put in the picture.
I hope that you will agree.

A great big heart for loving,
And eyes to look and see;
I'll draw two ears for listening,
To be like you and me.

I'll add two hands for helping,
A mouth for smiling, too.
Now count the many special things
That your best friend can do!

Draw a friend like this here.

Do you have a best friend?
What do you like to do together?

We are friends of Jesus.

Sharing Life

Name a friend.
What would your friend do if you were happy or unhappy?

What do you think Jesus would do if you were happy or unhappy?

What would life be like without friends?

You Can Learn
- Jesus cares for all people.
- Jesus healed people.
- We pray to Jesus, our Friend.

Our Faith

How do you know when someone is a good friend?
How is Jesus a good friend?

Jesus Cares for Everyone

Jesus loved and cared for everyone.
He hugged little children.
He healed people who were sick.
He helped people who were sad or afraid.
He cared for people who were poor.

Jesus cared for people who were not easy to love.
He even loved those whom other people hated.

Jesus said:
"Love your enemies.
Do good to those who hate you."
From Luke 6:27

Jesus is a really good Friend.
He is the best Friend we can have.

Sometimes we are sick or sad.
Sometimes we feel alone or afraid.
But we are never really alone.
We always have Jesus with us.
Jesus loves and cares for us.
Jesus is always our best Friend.

▸ **Color and pray**
Thank You, God, for giving us

Jesus.

How did Jesus treat everyone? Why is Jesus always our best Friend?

Our Faith (continued)

What did Jesus do for His friends?
What does Jesus do for us?

Jesus Healed the Sick

Sick people came to Jesus.
They believed in Him.
They asked if He would make them well again.
When Jesus touched them, they got better.
They were healed.

Read to me from the Bible

One time, a deaf man came to Jesus.
His friends asked Jesus to help him.
He believed in Jesus.
Jesus touched the man's ears.
He said, "Be opened!"
All at once, the man could hear.
Can you imagine how the man felt!
From Mark 7:32–35

Many people came to Jesus for help.
They believed in Jesus.
Jesus made them well.

Jesus wants all of us to be healthy.
He wants everyone to be happy.

◀ **Draw**
someone Jesus helped.
Tell about it.

What does Jesus do for people who believed in Him?
What will you do for Jesus?

93

Our Faith (continued)

How did Jesus help people? Do you ever ask Jesus to help you? Tell about it.

We Can Pray to Jesus

Prayer is talking and listening to God.

When we talk to Jesus, the Son of God, we are praying.

We can tell Jesus He is wonderful. We can thank Him for being our Friend.

We can ask Jesus to help us. When we do things that are wrong, we can tell Jesus we are sorry. Jesus always forgives us.

We can pray anywhere, anytime. We can pray in the morning, at night or before we eat.

Jesus always hears our prayers.

94

Coming to Faith

Circle your favorite times to pray.

Do you like to talk to Jesus? Why?

Can you ask Jesus to help others?

What will you ask for them?

Faith Summary

- Jesus cares for all people.
- Jesus heals people.
- We can pray to Jesus, our Friend.

Practicing Faith

Circle the picture that shows how you will try to help others as Jesus did.

Will you try to remember to say your morning and night prayers?

Faith Alive at Home

Reading the *Faith Summary* on page 95 will help your family to learn what was taught this week. Here are some things you may do to help your children know and live their faith.

Prayer corner

† If possible, help your child set up a prayer corner in his or her room. Place pictures of Jesus and His family in the corner. (If pictures are not available, help your child to draw them.) Reserve a special time in the day when you and your child can go to this corner to pray to Jesus. Pray this prayer: Thank You, God, for giving us Jesus as our best Friend.

Review Test

Read to me

Write the missing word on each line.

    healed   talking   Friend

1. Jesus ___ sick people.

   h_____

2. Praying is ___ to God.

   t_____

3. Jesus is my ___.

   F_____

4. When do you like to pray? Circle your answer.

       never   at night   anytime

Talk about friendship
Talk with your child about what a good friend Jesus is. Ask him or her how he or she can show friendship to others as Jesus did, within your family, at school, or in the neighborhood.

12 Jesus Is Our Teacher

Our Life

The families at Saint Rose's School have made a big photo album.

Look at their pictures.
How are the families showing they love one another?

Circle a picture of people being fair with others.
Circle people being peacemakers.

Tell a story about each picture.
How do you show your love?

Jesus brings Good News.

Sharing Life

How do you know when someone loves you?
What is the best way to show love for others?
What is the best way to show love for God?
Why is it sometimes difficult to love other people?

You Can Learn
- Jesus tells us God is our loving Parent.
- Jesus teaches us the Law of Love.
- Jesus tells us that God's love will last forever.

Our Faith

How do we show our love for others?
Who loves and cares for you?

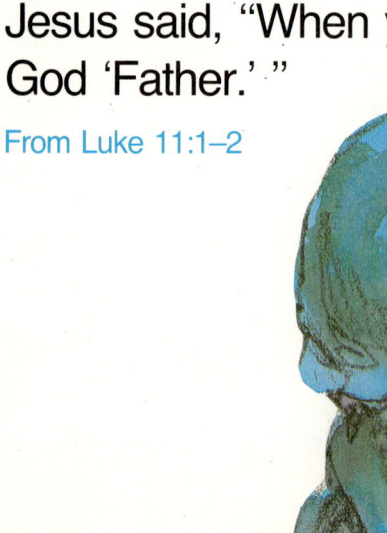

God Our Loving Parent

One day Jesus wanted to teach the people about God's love for them. He told them to think about their parents.

Parents love their children.
They care for them always.

Jesus told the people that God is like a loving Parent.
God loves us and cares for us, no matter what we do.

One day, Jesus' special friends said, "Teach us to pray."

Jesus said, "When you pray, call God 'Father.'"

From Luke 11:1–2

Faith Word
The **Our Father** is the prayer Jesus gave us.

Here is the prayer Jesus taught them.

☨ Our Father, who art in heaven,
hallowed be Thy name;
Thy Kingdom come;
Thy will be done on earth
as it is in heaven.
Give us this day our daily bread;
and forgive us our trespasses
as we forgive those
who trespass against us;
and lead us not into temptation,
but deliver us from evil. Amen.

◀ **Decorate**
the Our Father when you have learned it by heart.

How did Jesus teach us to pray?
When will you say the Our Father?

Our Faith (continued)

What does a loving parent do for a child?
What does it mean to really love someone?

The Law of Love
Jesus wants us to love God, to love others, and to love ourselves.

Read to me from the Bible

One day, a man came to Jesus.
He asked Jesus how God wants us to live.
Jesus said, "Love God above all things, and love other people as you love yourself."
From Mark 12:29–31

This is how God wants us to live. We call it the Law of Love. We are to show our love for God by loving others as we love ourselves.

Faith Word
The **Law of Love** is the way God wants us to live.

Of all the good things that we can do, Jesus said, love is the best thing of all.

What a happy world this would be if everyone loved God, loved all people, and loved themselves!

Gather
together with your friends. Say to the person next to you, "You are God's child. I love you."

Draw yourself and a friend on this page.

What do you think it means to love yourself?
Will you ask God to help you to love in this way?

103

Our Faith (continued)

How does God want us to live? Do you think God will love you forever? Why?

God's Love Lasts Forever

God's love for you is special. God will never stop loving you. God's love lasts forever.

Read to me from the Bible

Once Jesus said, "Look how God loves the birds. God feeds the birds. Look how God loves the flowers. God made them so beautiful."

Then Jesus said, "God loves you more than the birds and the flowers."
From Matthew 6:26–32

Coming to Faith

Tell how you can love
  God,
  your neighbor,
  yourself.

Color these words from the Our Father.

Our Father
who art in heaven.

† Pray the Our Father.

Faith Summary

- God is our loving Parent.
- We must love God, other people, and ourselves.
- God's love will last forever.

Practicing Faith

Color this banner.
Tell your friend what it means.

Love

God
People
Yourself

How will you show you love God?
How will you show you love others?
How will you love yourself?
When will you do these things?

Faith Alive at Home

Reading the *Faith Summary* on page 105 will help your family to learn what was taught this week. Here are some things you may do to help your children know and live their faith.

Review Test

Read to me

Write the missing word on each line.

　　Our Father　　　　Parent　　　　love

1. God is our loving ____.

P_____

2. Jesus taught us the ____ ____.

O_____ F_____

3. We must ____ God.

l_____

4. Circle how you live the Law of Love.

　　hit a friend　　　　hug a friend　　　　pray for a friend

Talk about the banner
Invite your child to show you the banner he or she decorated in class. Then ask your child to tell you what the words mean. Continue the activity by talking with him or her about different ways to love God, other people, and oneself. You might like to finish this activity by pointing out the difference between loving ourselves as God wants and selfishness.

✝ **Learning a prayer**
This week, your child was introduced to the prayer Jesus taught us—the Our Father. Go over this prayer with your child. Discuss with her or him the great joy that should be ours in being able to call God "Our Father."

107

13 Jesus Gives Us Himself

Our Life

Some Grandmas and Grandpas live far away. Here are ways to tell them we love them.

Phone a kiss.

Mail a hug.

Make a gift.

Write a card.

Circle one you can do. What else can you do?

Will it make your Grandma or Grandpa happy? How do you know?

Jesus is still with us.

Sharing Life

How do your friends remember you when you are away?

Put an X on the picture that shows what your friends do.

How do you feel when your friends remember you?

Does Jesus want you to remember Him? Tell why.

You Can Learn
- Jesus gives us Himself at the Last Supper.
- Jesus dies and rises from the dead.
- Jesus promises to give us a Helper, the Holy Spirit.

109

Our Faith

How do friends remember each other?
Whom do you want to remember?

The Last Supper

Jesus wanted us to remember Him.
Jesus wanted to be with us always.
This is what He did.

Read to me from the Bible

The night before Jesus died, He had a special meal with His friends. We call this meal the Last Supper.

During the meal, Jesus took bread.
He blessed it. He broke it.
He gave it to His friends and said, "This is My Body."

Jesus took a cup of wine.
He blessed it.
He gave it to His friends and said, "This is My Blood."

The bread and wine became the Body and Blood of Jesus.

Then Jesus said,
"Do this in memory of Me."
From Luke 22:14–20

Faith Word
Holy Communion is the Body and Blood of Jesus.

Jesus gives us the gift of Himself at Mass. He gives us His Body and Blood. We call the Body and Blood of Jesus "Holy Communion."

When you are ready, you can receive Jesus in Holy Communion.

◀ **Imagine**
you are at the Last Supper. Draw yourself at the table.

What was the special gift that Jesus gave us?
How will you thank Jesus for giving us the gift of Himself?

111

Our Faith (continued)

> Tell what happened at the Last Supper.
> How is Jesus always with His friends?

Jesus Dies and Rises

Today, we will learn what happened after the Last Supper.

Read to me from the Bible

After the Last Supper, Jesus and His friends went into a garden.
Jesus prayed. Some soldiers came and took Him away.
They said Jesus had taught, "I am God's Son!"
They did not believe Jesus' words.
They said Jesus had to die.
From Matthew 26:36–66

Jesus was nailed to a cross. Jesus' Mother and some friends were by the cross. They stayed with Him until He died.
From John 19:18–30

Two friends of Jesus put His body
in a tomb. It was very dark.
Everyone was sad.

On Easter Sunday Jesus' friend,
Mary Magdalene, went to the tomb.
Jesus' body was not there. There
was a man by the tomb.
The man said, "Mary!"
Mary looked at Him. It was Jesus!

Jesus said, "Go tell My friends that
I have risen from the dead."
From John 20:14–17

Mary did what Jesus said.
Jesus' friends were happy that
He was alive.

Jesus is alive and with us today.
Jesus is with us always.

Tell what happened after
the Last Supper.
What will you tell Jesus to show
you are happy He is with you?

Our Faith (continued)

Tell the story of Easter Sunday. What do you think happened to Jesus' friends after Easter?

The Holy Spirit

Jesus stayed with His friends for a while.
Then it was time for Him to go back to God in heaven.

Jesus knew His friends would need help.
He said, "Do not be afraid. I will not leave you alone."

From John 14:16

Jesus promised to send His friends a Helper to remind them of all He had told them.

The Helper that Jesus sent was the Holy Spirit, the third Person of the Blessed Trinity.

God the Holy Spirit helps us today to live as friends of Jesus.

Coming to Faith

Tell one of these stories:

Holy Thursday   Good Friday

Easter Sunday

Use the pictures in your book to help you.

How is Jesus with us today?
How can you show your thanks to Jesus for what He did?

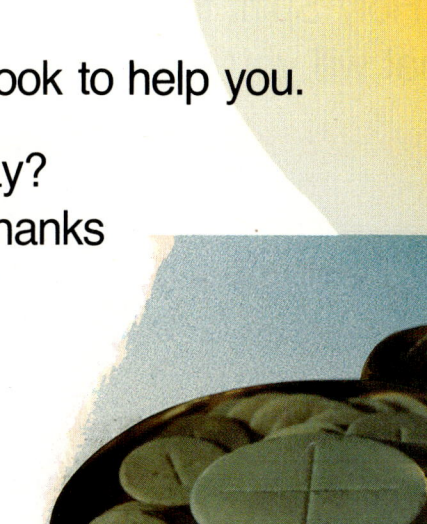

Faith Summary

- Jesus gives us the gift of Himself in Holy Communion.
- Jesus dies and rises from the dead.
- Jesus promises to give a Helper, the Holy Spirit.

Practicing Faith

Draw a gift you will give Jesus.

When do you need Jesus to help you? How will you ask Him? Will you ask the Holy Spirit to help you? When? What will you say?

Faith Alive at Home

Reading the *Faith Summary* on page 115 will help your family to learn what was taught this week. Here are some things you may do to help your children know and live their faith.

Pray together
Talk with your child about the great love Jesus showed by giving His life for each of us. Impress upon your child the fact that this shows how much God loves us.

Review Test

Read to me

Write the missing word on each line.

died　　　　Holy Communion　　　　Last Supper

1. Jesus gave us Himself at the ___ ___.

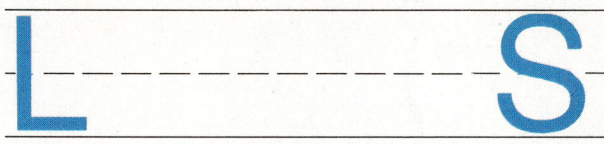

   L_____ S_____

2. ___ ___ is Jesus' Body and Blood.

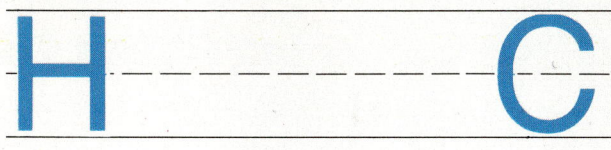

   H_____ C_____

3. Jesus ___ for me.

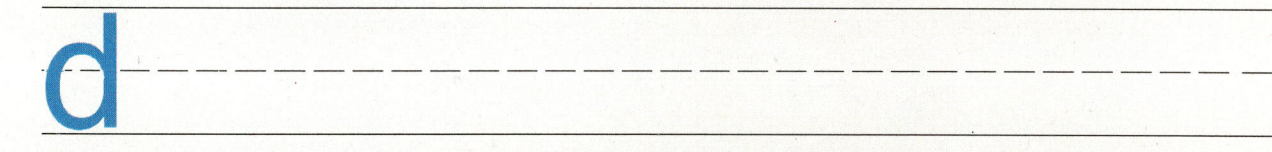

   d_____

4. Circle how you feel because Jesus is risen.

   happy　　　　sad　　　　angry

Say this prayer together with your child.

† Thank You, Jesus, for giving us Yourself and for promising to help us always.

The Last Supper
Help your child to make a drawing showing what Jesus did at the Last Supper. Have him or her tell you or a friend about the drawing.

14 Advent

Our Life

Are you waiting for something special right now?
Does it feel like it will never come?
What are you waiting for?
Tell your class about it.

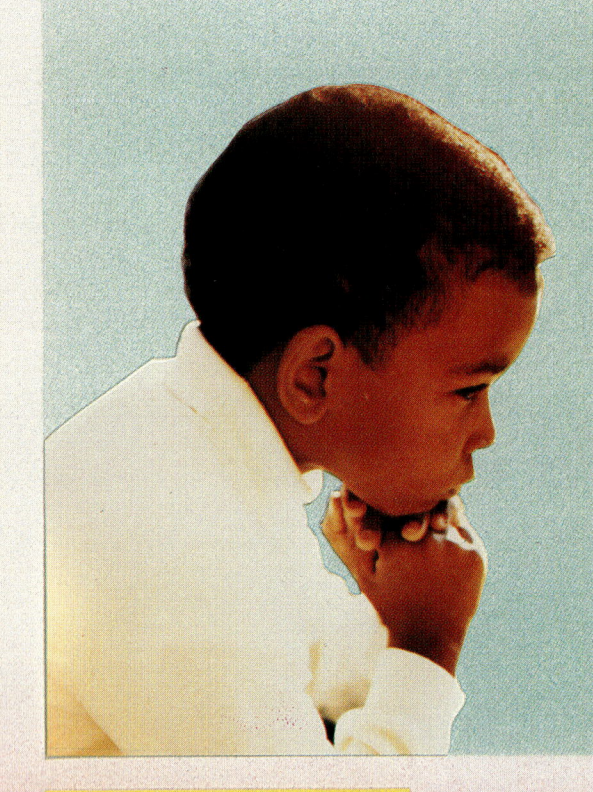

Sharing Life

Imagine someone wants to give you a gift.
What would you ask for?
How would you feel if you had to wait nine months for your gift?

Our Faith

The Bible tells us the story of how the first man and woman said no to God. God did not stop loving them. God promised to send God's Son to show people how to live as friends of God.

The people waited many, many years for God's Son.
While they waited, they got ready. Finally Jesus was born in Bethlehem.

Each year we remember and celebrate Jesus' birthday on Christmas. We continue to wait until Jesus will come again. Advent is the name we give to our waiting time.

We do things to get ready for the birthday of Jesus. We try to be kind and fair. Look at the pictures. Circle the things you can do.

Coming to Faith

Think about some things people can do to get ready to celebrate the birthday of Jesus on Christmas day.

Share your ideas with your class.

Practicing Faith

How will you get ready for Christmas?

Draw something that you will do for each week on your Advent calendar.

Advent Calendar

First Week	Second Week	Third Week	Fourth Week

✝ Advent Prayer Service

Leader: God, you promised the people long ago to send us Your Son. Now, during Advent, we pray:

All: Come to us, Jesus.

Leader: We wait for Christmas, not thinking of ourselves, but thinking of Jesus.

All: Come to us, Jesus.

Leader: Help us to live as your friends, not only during Advent, but all of the time.

All: Come to us, Jesus.

Faith Alive at Home

Make a family Advent calendar on which the entire family can record Advent acts. Talk with your child about doing something for Jesus each day.

15 Christmas

Our Life

What do you like best about Christmas? Tell about it.

Sharing Life

Imagine you are at Bethlehem on the first Christmas.
Tell what you see and hear.

Our Faith

A Christmas Play

Narrator: In those days, a letter went out from the King that all the people should be counted. Mary and Joseph went to Bethlehem to be counted.

Joseph: Mary, we are almost there. You must be tired. Let's stop at the inn. (knocks at the door)

Innkeeper: What do you want?

Joseph: We need a place to rest.

Innkeeper: There is no room for you here. You can stay in the stable in the back.

Narrator: The stable was filled with many animals. There were cows, donkeys, and sheep.

Sheep: Baa! Baa! Baa!

Narrator: During the night, Jesus was born. In a nearby field shepherds were caring for their sheep. Suddenly a bright light filled the sky. Angels appeared to them.

Angels: Do not be afraid. We have Good News. The Savior is born. You will find a baby in a stable in Bethlehem.

Narrator: The shepherds went to Bethlehem. They found Mary, Joseph, and the Baby Jesus in a stable.

All Sing "Silent Night."

Coming to Faith

What is your favorite part of the Christmas story?
Act out the story with some friends.

Practicing Faith

Jesus is with us today.
How will you show your love for
Jesus on Christmas day and every day?

Draw it here.

✝ Christmas Prayer Service

All: Sing the hymn "Silent Night."

Reader: (Read Luke 2:7–19.)

Leader: Jesus was born in Bethlehem.

All: Glory to God.

Leader: The shepherds came to visit Jesus.

All: Glory to God.

Leader: Let us welcome Jesus into our hearts today and always.

All: Come, Jesus, come. Sing "Silent Night."

Faith Alive at Home

If possible, spend some time before Christmas praying the above prayer service.

16 Unit II Review

Jesus is part of our human family.

Jesus was human like us. He laughed and played with His friends. He loved and cared for them. At times He was sad or tired. Jesus did the things we do.

Jesus is God's own Son.

Jesus showed the people how much God loved them. Jesus showed by what He did and said that He was God's own Son.

Jesus is our Friend and Teacher.

Jesus showed the people how to love and care for one another. What a happy world this would be if everyone loved God, loved all people, and loved themselves.

Jesus gave Himself for us.

The night before Jesus died He shared a special meal, the Last Supper, with His friends. The next day, Good Friday, Jesus died for all His friends. On Easter Sunday, Jesus rose from the dead. Jesus is alive and with us today.

Unit 11 Test

Read to me

Write in the missing word.

> God's   love   alive   human

1. Jesus is part of our ____ family.

   h

2. Jesus is ____ own Son.

   G

3. Jesus said ____ is the best thing of all.

   l

4. Jesus is ____ and with us today.

   a

5. Draw what you would like to do to make this world a happy place.

17 First Semester Review

God made all things.

God made the world wonderful. God created plants, animals, and people. People are special in God's world. They can know and love and create.

God gave people a share in God's own life. This share in God's life is called grace.

God always loves and cares for us. God wants us to love and care for others.

Jesus is God's greatest gift to us.

Jesus is God's own Son. He shows us how much God loves us.

Jesus gave us the Law of Love. He told us to love God, others, and ourselves. Jesus is our best friend.

Jesus died on Good Friday and rose from the dead on Easter Sunday. He is alive and with us today.

First Semester Test

Read to me

Circle the correct answer.

1. God ____ to be with us always.
   promises   hopes

2. ____ is God's own Son.
   Jesus   Joseph

3. The ____ is God's Holy Book.
   Bible   Reader

4. God gives people ____ life.
   human   animal

5. ____ is the second Person of the Blessed Trinity.
   God   Jesus

6. We call God's own life in us ____.
   grace   life

7. Draw one thing you will do to live the Law of Love.

18 The Holy Spirit

Our Life

Here are some photographs from José Ramirez's family photo album.

Look at José being a helper.

Who is José helping?
How is José helping?

José loves being a helper.
José loves being helped, too.

Look at José being helped.

Who is helping José?
How is José being helped?

We have a Helper—
the Holy Spirit.

Name some times when you need help.
Who helps you?
How do they help you?

Sharing Life

Why do we need helpers?
How can you help others?

You Can Learn

- The Holy Spirit came to the friends of Jesus.
- The Holy Spirit helped the friends of Jesus.
- The Holy Spirit helped Jesus' friends to be His Church.

Our Faith

Who helps you every day?
Why do we sometimes need help?

The Holy Spirit Comes

Jesus knew that after He left them His friends would need a Helper. He told them, "I will send you a Helper. The Holy Spirit will help you remember all that I have said."

From John 14:26

Here's the story of how Jesus kept His promise.

Read to me from the Bible

The friends of Jesus were waiting for the Helper Jesus had promised. Mary, the Mother of Jesus, was with them.

Suddenly they heard a loud noise like a wind blowing. They saw flames of fire in the air.

The Holy Spirit had come! The friends of Jesus were filled with the Holy Spirit.

Then Jesus' friends ran out of the room into the street. They told all the people gathered there the Good News of Jesus.

From Acts 2:2–6

Faith Word
The **Holy Spirit** is God, the third Person of the Blessed Trinity.

God, the Holy Spirit, helped the friends of Jesus to remember everything Jesus had said and done.

The Holy Spirit is with us today. The Holy Spirit helps us to live as Jesus taught us.

◀ **Act out**

what happened when the Holy Spirit came?

How does the Holy Spirit help you? What will you ask the Holy Spirit to help you do today?

133

Our Faith (continued)

Who is the Helper Jesus gave His friends?

Is it sometimes difficult to do the right thing? Why?

The Holy Spirit the Helper

After Jesus went away, the friends of Jesus were afraid that they might be killed, too. The Holy Spirit helped them not to be afraid.

The Holy Spirit helped the friends of Jesus in many ways. The Holy Spirit helped them to pray every day. The Holy Spirit was with them when they shared the Bread and Wine, the Body and Blood of Christ. The Holy Spirit helped them to remember that Jesus wanted them to love others. The Holy Spirit helped them to be peacemakers.

The friends of Jesus shared what they had. No one was hungry. Each had a place to stay.

Everyone said, "See how these Christians love one another." Christians are followers of Jesus.

Faith Word
Christians are followers of Jesus Christ.

The Holy Spirit helps you, too.
The Holy Spirit helps you to live as a friend of Jesus.

▶ **Write and learn**

"See how these Christians love one another."

What did the Holy Spirit do for the friends of Jesus? How will you ask the Holy Spirit to help you?

Our Faith (continued)

What is a Christian? How can the Holy Spirit help you?

The Church Begins

The Holy Spirit helped the first Christians to tell the Good News of Jesus to everyone.

More and more people believed in Jesus Christ. They came together as Jesus' Church.

The Church is Jesus and His baptized friends joined together by the Holy Spirit.

The Holy Spirit helped the friends of Jesus be His Church. The Holy Spirit still helps the Church today.

You are a follower of Jesus. You are a member of His Church. The Holy Spirit will help you to live as a Christian.

Coming to Faith

Tell some of the things the Holy Spirit does to help us live as friends of Jesus.

Circle two pictures that show how the Holy Spirit helps us.

Tell how the Holy Spirit is helping.

When do you need the help of the Holy Spirit most?

Faith Summary

- The Holy Spirit came to the friends of Jesus.
- The Holy Spirit helped the Church to begin.
- The Holy Spirit helps us today.

Practicing Faith

Circle the help you need from the Holy Spirit today.

to pray   to love others   to be fair

When will you ask for this help?

Color and pray

Holy Spirit

† Holy Spirit, help me today in all I think, and do, and say!

Faith Alive at Home

Reading the *Faith Summary* on page 137 will help your family to learn what was taught this week. Here are some things you may do to help your children know and live their faith.

Talking about the Holy Spirit
Ask your child to share with you what he or she learned about the Holy Spirit this week.

Praying together
You may wish to pray this prayer to the Holy Spirit together as a family.

† Come, Holy Spirit, help us to remember what Jesus said and did. Help us to live as friends of Jesus. Help us to be good members of Jesus' Church. Amen.

Review Test

Read to me

Color the circle next to each correct answer.

1. The Holy Spirit helps ____.

    ○ me   ○ animals   ○ plants

2. The Holy Spirit helps Jesus' friends to ____.

    ○ eat   ○ jump   ○ pray

3. A ____ follows Jesus.

    ○ Holy Spirit   ○ Christian   ○ friend

4. Draw or tell how you will help someone today.

Drawing a picture
Talk with your child about some of the times he or she might need the special help of the Holy Spirit. Invite your child to make a drawing of one of these times.

Talk about the drawing with your child. You might ask how the Holy Spirit can help in that situation. Then share with him or her ways in which the Holy Spirit has helped you in your life.

19 The Church Is for Everyone

Our Life

Read to me

"Emergency meeting at the beavers' lodge," trumpeted the elephant all over the zoo. Hurrying to the lodge, the animals found the beavers nervously thumping their tails.

"We have a problem. Our dam needs repair, but there is no wood available," said the beavers.

"I have an idea," said the giraffe. "The zoo has many trees with dry, dead branches. I can reach up and pull them down."

"Good idea," said the other animals. "We'll be a team, everyone playing a part."

"We'll carry away the shavings," offered the ants and chipmunks. "I can carry the big branches with my trunk," cried the elephant.

"What can we do?" asked the frogs.

"You can cheer us on," replied the thankful beavers. "Everyone knows frogs have wonderful voices."

All the animals set to work as the frogs sang in their deep voices,
"You do your part,
I'll do mine.
Working together
It will turn out fine."

The Church of Jesus is for everyone.

What did each animal in the group do to help the beavers?

What team or group do you belong to? What do you do together? Do you like to work together?

Sharing Life

Why do people sometimes need to work together?
Why should friends of Jesus work together?

You Can Learn

- Paul joins the Church.
- We are part of the Church.
- The Church is for everyone.

141

Our Faith

What happens when friends work together?
How do the friends of Jesus work together?

Paul Joins the Church

Jesus' friends told many people about Him. The Holy Spirit helped the people to believe in Jesus.

The new friends of Jesus wanted to join the group of Jesus' followers. They were baptized. They became Christians. They became part of Jesus' Church.

One of Jesus' special friends was a man named Paul. Paul was not always Jesus' friend.

At first he was mean to people who were followers of Jesus. But then the Holy Spirit helped him know that Jesus was really God's own Son.

From that time on, Paul traveled everywhere telling people about Jesus. He became a great leader in the Church.

Paul helped people know that the Church of Jesus was for everyone. Anyone who believed in Jesus and wanted to be His follower could be baptized.

What did people have to do to belong to the Church of Jesus? Tell how you became a Christian.

Our Faith (continued)

What did people have to do to join Jesus' Church?
How can other people know that you are a friend of Jesus?

You Are Part of the Church

Jesus teaches us how to live as His followers. Jesus said, "Love one another just as I love you."
John 15:12

When Jesus saw that people were hungry, He fed them.
If people were lonely,
He became their friend.

When Jesus saw sick people, He helped them get better.
Jesus was fair to everyone.
He helped people to live in peace.

We are friends of Jesus.
We belong to the Church.

We try to show our love for one another. We try to be fair and to make peace. That is what it means to be a follower of Jesus.

If someone in your class forgets to bring lunch, what can you do?

If a new classmate is lonely and needs a friend, what can you do?

If someone is not being fair to someone else what can you do? When people fight, what can you do?

◀ **Trace and wear** a button that says, "I am a friend of Jesus."

I am a friend of **Jesus**

What does a follower of Jesus do? How does Jesus want you to live? Will you?

145

Our Faith (continued)

How do the followers of Jesus treat one another?
Who can be a follower of Jesus?

The Church Is for Everyone

Jesus invites everyone to belong to His Church. Everyone in the Church is important.

Our Holy Father, the Pope, is the leader of the whole Church.

Our bishops and priests help care for the Church. Many other people help, too.

Some take care of the sick.
Some are teachers.
Some are mothers and fathers.
All of us try to help one another.

The Church needs you.

Coming to Faith

What do you think it means to be a member of Jesus' Church?

How do the friends of Jesus help one another in the Church?

Write the name of our Holy Father, the Pope, here.

_____
_____

Write your Bishop's name here.

_____
_____

Name one of your priests. Write his name here.

_____
_____

Faith Summary

- The Holy Spirit helped the Church to grow.
- We are part of the Church.
- We try to treat others the way Jesus would treat them.

Practicing Faith

Put an X next to each sentence that shows how you will love.

☐ I will be a good friend to my schoolmates.

☐ I will try not to be mean to anyone.

☐ I will share my toys with my friends.

☐ I will try to be fair to everyone.

☐ I will try to be a peacemaker.

Circle the sentence that tells what you will do today.

Faith Alive at Home

Reading the *Faith Summary* on page 147 will help your family to learn what was taught this week. Here are some things you may do to help your children know and live their faith.

Helping in the parish
Each person in your parish has different talents. Discuss with your child the different gifts that people share to make the parish a special place. Help your child understand what he or she can do to make the parish a better place to be in.

148

Review Test

Read to me

Color the circle next to each correct answer.

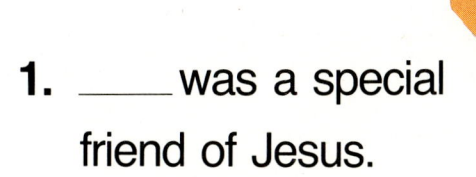

1. ____ was a special friend of Jesus.

   ○ Max ○ Paul ○ Ann

2. We are part of the ____.

   ○ circus ○ sea ○ Church

3. The Church of Jesus is for ____.

   ○ Paul ○ everyone ○ no one

4. Today I will ____.

   ○ be mean ○ be a peacemaker ○ fight

Praying together
Share with your child a prayer of thanks for belonging to the Church. You may wish to use the following prayer:

† Jesus, thank You for inviting me to belong to Your Church. Help me to do my part by following Your way.

20 The Church Celebrates Baptism

Our Life

Read to me

Janie Antonelli was all smiles. It was Baby Tony's baptismal day. Janie was so proud to be sitting in the front pew of the church. She was so happy when her mother slipped one of her fingers into her brother Tony's tiny hand.

After a while Janie's mother said, "Janie, we have to take Tony up to be baptized now." The whole family went up around the baptismal font.

Janie's eyes followed Baby Tony. She saw the priest pour water on Tony's head. She listened to all the words. When the baptism was over, the priest said, "Anthony is now a child of God. Let us welcome him into the Church." Everyone clapped.

Turning to her mother, Janie said, "Mommy, Tony is a child of God!"

Her mother smiled. She said, "Yes, Janie, and so are you."

Janie was excited. "I never thought of it," she said. "I am a child of God, too." Janie smiled back at her mother.

Have you been baptized? What do you think it means to be a child of God?

We belong to God.

Sharing Life

Tell why you think your family wanted you to become a child of God.

Are you happy to be a child of God? Why?

How should God's children live?

You Can Learn

- We celebrate Baptism.
- Baptism makes us children of God.
- We live like Jesus because we are baptized.

Our Faith

Do you know when you were baptized?
What do you think happened on that day?

We Celebrate Baptism

Jesus wants us all to be God's children.
He wants us to have God's own life and love.

When we are baptized, we become God's own children.
We receive God's own life and love.
We become part of the Church.

Baptism gives us God's own life and love.
The Holy Spirit helps us to live as Jesus taught us.

Faith Word
Baptism gives us God's own life and love.

You are baptized.
You are God's child.
The Holy Spirit is with you.
You share in God's life.
You belong to the Church.

You try to live the way Jesus taught.

◀ **Draw** yourself in this picture.

Are you happy that you are baptized? Why?
What will you do to show that you are happy?

Our Faith (continued)

Why do families celebrate when they have a child baptized? What happens when someone is baptized?

Baptism Makes Us God's Children

Catholic parents want their babies to become children of God. They want their babies to be baptized.

They bring the baby to the church. The priest and the people welcome them. Everyone prays for the baby and the family.

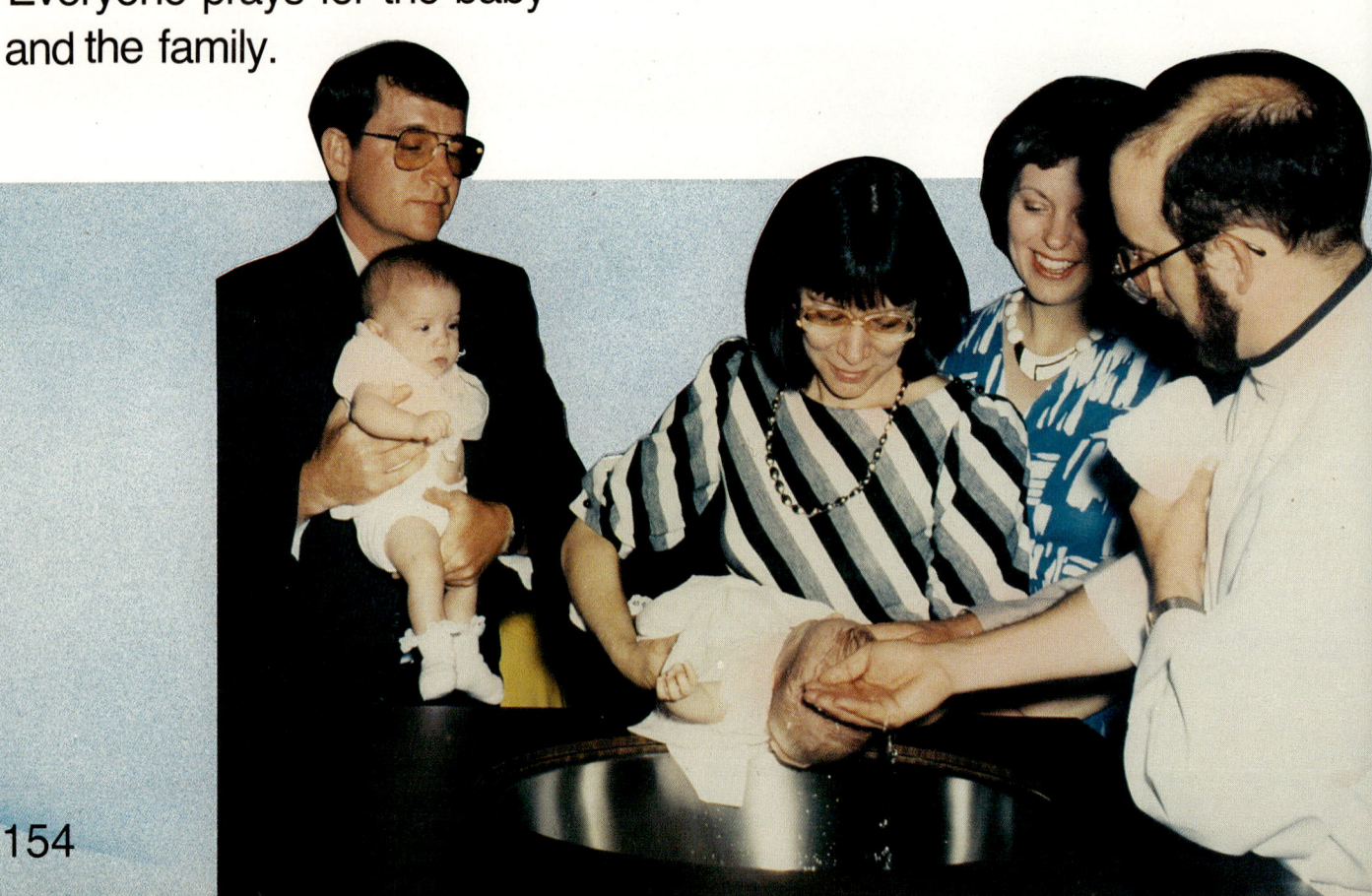

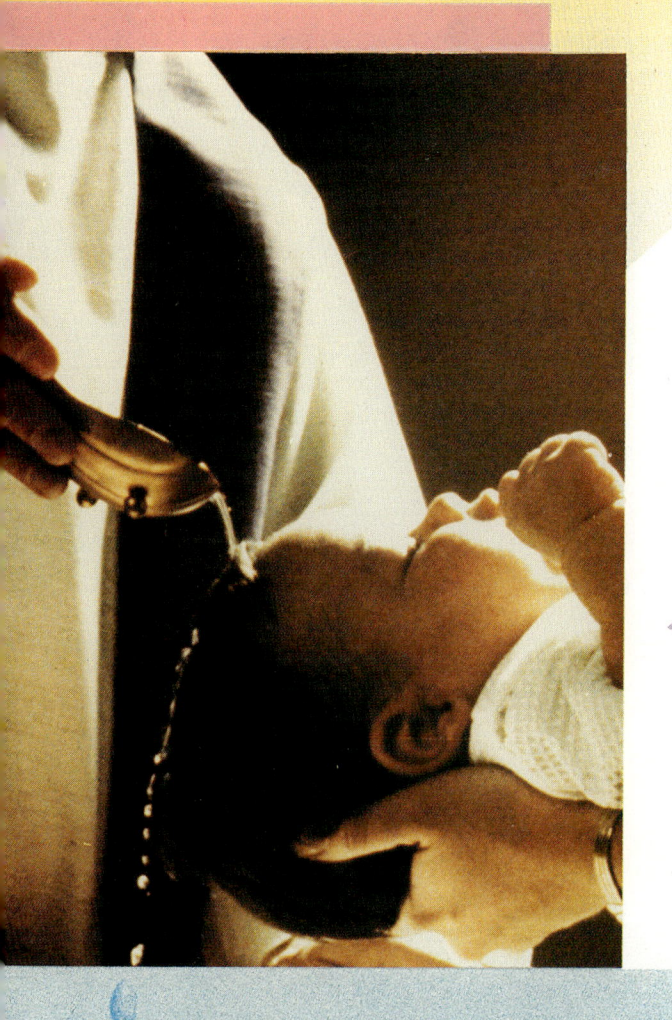

The priest pours water over the baby's head. He says,
† "I baptize you
in the name of the Father,
and of the Son,
and of the Holy Spirit."

The baby now has God's special life of grace. The baby is now a child of God and a member of Jesus' Church.

◀ **Act out**
a Baptism. Paste a picture here.

How do you know you are God's child?
How does that make you feel?

155

Our Faith (continued)

What does the priest do at a Baptism?
Tell something you can do because you are baptized.

We Live Like Jesus

When the first Christians were baptized, they wanted everyone to know the Good News of Jesus.

The Holy Spirit helped them to tell others about Jesus.

The Holy Spirit helped them to live as Jesus did.

We are baptized.
We tell everyone about Jesus.

The Holy Spirit helps us to live as friends of Jesus.

Coming to Faith

Are you happy you are baptized?
How can you show it?

What happens when you are baptized?
Color the answer below.

I become

God's child

Faith Summary

- We share in God's own life when we are baptized.
- Baptism makes us children of God and members of Jesus' Church.
- We live like Jesus because we are baptized.

Practicing Faith

When you go to church the next time, make the Sign of the Cross and bless yourself with the holy water. Say thank you to God that you are baptized and are God's child.

Circle one thing you will do this week to show that you are God's child.

Faith Alive at Home

Reading the *Faith Summary* on page 157 will help your family to learn what was taught this week. Here are some things you may do to help your children know and live their faith.

† **Sign of the Cross**
You might want to recall your feelings about your child's baptismal day. Share these feelings with your child. You might make the Sign of the Cross as you bless yourself and your child with holy water. Explain to your child that this reminds us of the water used on our Baptism day.

Review Test

Color the circle next to each correct answer.

1. You became God's special child when you were ____.

    ○ baptized ○ born ○ singing

2. The priest uses ____ to baptize.

    ○ sand ○ water ○ sugar

3. Because we are baptized, we live like ____.

    ○ plants ○ birds ○ Jesus

4. In Baptism we receive God's ____.

    ○ cross ○ life ○ body

5. How will you show you are God's child?

    ○ fight ○ help ○ steal

---

† Quiet prayer
Talk with your child about God's life within us. Teach him or her to reflect quietly on this wonder of God's love. You might like to lead him or her in the following reflective prayer.

Close your eyes.
Think quietly for a few minutes about God's life in you.
Thank God in your own words for this wonderful gift.

21 The Church Celebrates
(The Mass Begins)

Our Life

Read to me

The beavers were so happy. All the animals in the zoo had worked together to help the beavers repair their dam.

"Let's have a celebration to show how much we love our friends," cried the beavers. So Wally, the leader of the beavers, sent an invitation to each animal in the zoo.

All the animals were so happy to receive the invitations. Harold the elephant raised his big trunk to trumpet his joy. Cornelia the giraffe picked the prettiest flowers.

Arnie the ant scurried here and there to tell his ant friends to bring a lot of food. The monkeys swung from tree to tree to make sure no one was left behind. Everyone was invited.

Harriet and Lionel, the frogs, began clearing their throats and practicing all the songs they knew. Finally, the big day arrived. Everything was ready. Everyone came.

We celebrate the Mass.

What did each of the animals do to get ready for the celebration?
What is your family's favorite celebration?
What do you do to help?

Sharing Life

Imagine the best celebration ever.
Who would be there?
What would there be to eat?
What would you wear?
What exciting things would you do?

You Can Learn

- Jesus gives us the Mass.
- We see and hear many things at Mass.
- How the Mass begins.

Our Faith

What makes a good celebration?
Who comes to your favorite celebration?

Jesus Gives Us the Mass

The friends of Jesus have a special meal to celebrate together. We call it the Mass. Here is how the Mass began.

The night before He died, Jesus had a special meal with His friends. It was the last supper He had with them.

They sang songs and prayed together. They read from God's Holy Word in the Bible.

Read to me from the Bible

Then Jesus took bread.
He thanked God for it.
He gave it to His friends.
He said, "This is My Body."
He took a cup of wine. He said, "This is My Blood. Do this in memory of Me."
From Luke 22:19

Faith Word
The **Mass** is the special celebration in which we hear God's Word and share the Body and Blood of Jesus.

The first Christians met for their special celebration. They listened to God's Holy Word in the Bible. They brought gifts of bread and wine. They received the Body and Blood of Jesus.

Today Catholics meet for our special celebration of the Mass. We listen to God's holy word in the Bible. We do what Jesus did at the Last Supper. We receive the Body and Blood of Jesus in Holy Communion.

When do you go to Mass? What will you do at Mass?

Our Faith (continued)

What is the Mass?
Do you like to go to Mass?
Why or why not?

The Mass

Jesus is with us each time we celebrate the Mass.
We gather with our family and friends for Mass in our parish church on Sunday or on Saturday evening.

The priest, our leader at Mass, wears special clothes called vestments.

A beautiful cloth is put on the holy table. We call the table the altar.

A special plate and cup are used for the bread and wine.

Two candles are lighted on or near the altar.

Faith Word
The **altar** is the holy table where Mass is celebrated.

We pray together at Mass.

Sometimes we pray out loud. Sometimes we pray in our hearts. Sometimes we pray by joining in the singing. We pray standing, or sitting, or kneeling.

Draw
what you like to do at Mass.

What do you see and hear when you go to Mass?
What will you do at Mass?

Our Faith (continued)

What do you like best about going to Mass?
What do you do at Mass?

The Mass Begins

Mass is our great celebration together. We all have a part to play in the Mass.

The Mass begins when the priest comes into the church. We stand and join in the singing. This shows we are all God's people.

With the priest, we make the Sign of the Cross. The priest welcomes us. We hear him say,
"The Lord be with you."
We answer,
"And also with you."

The priest invites us to ask God and one another for forgiveness. Then we join with the priest to tell God how wonderful God is. We pray for one another and ask God for what we need.

Coming to Faith

Circle all the words that are part of the Mass.

Body   priest   Blood

prayer   Last Supper   Jesus

Tell your friends what you circled. Explain why.

What are your favorite parts of our Mass celebration?

Why do we celebrate the Mass?

Faith Summary

- The friends of Jesus shared a special meal, the Last Supper.
- Today, we call this special meal the Mass.
- At Mass we celebrate that Jesus is with us.

Practicing Faith

Will you promise God to go to Mass this Sunday or Saturday evening?

Write out and decorate your promise.

My Promise

1. I will go to the _____ _____ _____ o'clock Mass.

2. I will go with _____ _____ _____.

3. I will thank God for _____ _____ _____.

Faith Alive at Home

Reading the *Faith Summary* on page 167 will help your family to learn what was taught this week. Here are some things you may do to help your children know and live their faith.

Talk about Mass
Perhaps you would like to point out to your child the things you see and hear at Mass. Encourage your child to participate as fully as possible in the Mass.

Review Test

Color the circle next to each correct answer.

1. The celebration of Jesus' Last Supper is called ____.

    ○ Good Friday   ○ Christmas   ○ Mass

2. The special table is the ____.

    ○ altar   ○ candle   ○ cross

3. Our leader at Mass is the ____.

    ○ people   ○ priest   ○ me

4. How does Mass begin?

5. Circle all your favorite ways to take part in the Mass.

    sing   pray   kneel

    stand   sit   read along

† **The Lord's Prayer**
You might like to pray the Our Father with your child. Pray it slowly and reverently.

169

22 The Church Celebrates
(The Mass Continues)

Our Life

Look at this drawing of a parish church.

Circle and name each of the things we see when our parish celebrates Mass.

What is your parish church like?

Color the drawing. Make it look like your parish church.

What do you like best about your parish church?

170

We all have a part in the Mass.

Sharing Life

Why is the Mass a wonderful celebration?

What is your part in the celebration?

What is the best way for you to take part in celebrating the Mass?

You Can Learn

- At Mass, we listen to God's word.
- Our gifts to God become Jesus.
- Jesus comes to us in Holy Communion.

Our Faith

What happens when Mass begins?
Today we will learn what happens next at Mass.

We Listen to God's Word

At Mass we listen to God's word.
We try to be good listeners.

When the reader says,
"This is the word of the Lord."
We answer,
"Thanks be to God."

Then we listen to the Gospel.
The Gospel is the Good News, or stories of Jesus.
Jesus has given us Good News.
The Good News is that God loves us.

After the Gospel, the priest says,
"This is the gospel of the Lord."
We answer,
"Praise to you, Lord Jesus Christ."

We sit and listen while the priest talks to us about the readings from the Bible.

Faith Word
The **Gospel** is the Good News of Jesus.

After listening to God's word from the Bible, the priest explains God's word to the people. Then we pray a prayer that tells what we believe. We call this our Creed.

After this, we pray for others.

After each prayer we answer, "Lord, hear our prayer."

Write

"Lord, hear our prayer."

For whom would you like to pray at Mass?
What will you say?

173

Our Faith (continued)

Whom do we pray for at Mass?
What gifts can you bring to God at Mass?

Our Gifts to God Become Jesus

Some people are asked to bring our gifts of bread and wine to the altar. This shows that we want to offer ourselves to God.

The priest prepares our gifts to be offered to God.

We answer,
"Blessed be God forever."

Then the priest says the words Jesus said at the Last Supper.

He takes the bread in his hands and says,
" This is my body which will be given up for you."

He takes the cup of wine and says,
" This is the cup of my blood . . ."

Through the words of the priest and the power of the Holy Spirit, the Bread and Wine become Jesus Himself.

What happens to our gifts of bread and wine at Mass? Would you like to bring the gifts up to the altar someday? Why?

Our Faith (continued)

What happens to the bread and wine at Mass?
Would you like Jesus to be with you always? Why?

Holy Communion
During the Mass the bread and wine become Jesus Himself. Jesus is our Bread of Life. When we are ready, we can receive Jesus in Holy Communion. When we receive the Body and Blood of Jesus Christ, we say, "Amen."

At the end of Mass, the priest blesses us. He tells us,
"Go in peace to love and serve the Lord."

We answer,
"Thanks be to God."

The Mass is ended.
We go in peace to love God and one another.

Coming to Faith

Write the missing word on each line.

| Jesus | bread and wine | Bible |

1. At Mass, we listen to readings from the _____.

2. We offer gifts of _____.

3. The bread and wine become _____.

Faith Summary
- We listen to God's word at Mass.
- Our gifts to God become Jesus.
- We receive Jesus in Holy Communion.

Practicing Faith

Jesus is with us at Mass.

Here are some of the things that happen at Mass.

Tell someone what is happening in each picture.
Is there someone you can invite to Mass this Sunday? Who will it be?

Faith Alive at Home

Reading the *Faith Summary* on page 177 will help your family to learn what was taught this week. Here are some things you may do to help your children know and live their faith.

Visit the church
You might like to take your child to visit the church before Mass begins next weekend. Show your child the altar and the lectern where the Bible is placed. Point out the candles and the statues.

178

Review Test

Color the circle next to each correct answer.

1. The ____ is the Good News of Jesus.

    ○ singing   ○ Gospel   ○ loving

2. Our gifts to God become ____.

    ○ Jesus   ○ Holy Spirit   ○ me

3. At Mass we can pray for ____.

    ○ everyone   ○ Jesus   ○ Billy

4. At Mass the bread and wine become ____.

    ○ Mary   ○ Jesus   ○ Paul

5. What will you do to show you are a peacemaker?

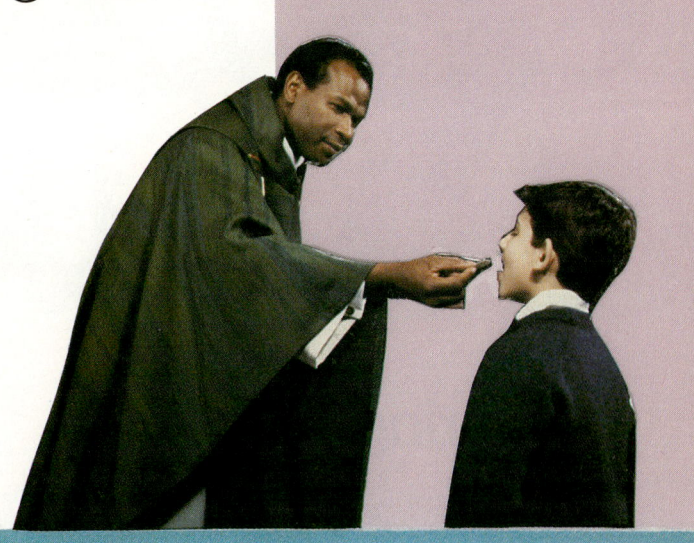

† **Praying with your child**
Show your child the holy-water font. Invite him or her to bless himself or herself with holy water. Be sure he or she makes the Sign of the Cross slowly and reverently. Then bless yourself.

23 Lent

Our Life

Think of something wonderful that someone who loves you has done for you.
Tell about it.

Sharing Life

Why did he or she do this wonderful thing for you?

Our Faith

During Lent we remember what Jesus did for us.
We remember Jesus died for us.
We remember Jesus rose from the dead.

During Lent, we try in a special way to love others as Jesus does.

The Church gives us a prayer to say especially during Lent.
It is called the Way of the Cross.
It helps us to remember how much Jesus loves us. It helps us remember to love others.
There is a short Way of the Cross for you to pray on text page 183.

Coming to Faith

How did Jesus show His love for us?
During Lent what kind things can
you do to show love?

Practicing Faith

Make a Way of the Cross for Lent.
Cut out 14 pieces of paper like
this one.

> † I will be kind to _____ _____
> _____ _____ .
> _____ _____
> _____ _____ .

On each paper or "station" write a
kind act you will do for someone.

Faith Alive at Home

You might like to spend a few minutes
talking with your child about the pictures
in this lesson.

✝ The Way of the Cross

Leader: Jesus was told He must die. Everyone left Him alone.

All: Jesus, help us to remember You.

Leader: Jesus had to carry His cross. O Jesus, sometimes things are hard to do.

All: Jesus, help us to do hard things.

Leader: Jesus met Mary His mother.

All: Jesus, help us to go to Mary, too!

Leader: Jesus fell down. The cross was so heavy and Jesus was so tired.

All: Jesus, help us never to give up.

Leader: Everything was quiet. Jesus was on the cross. Jesus said to God the Father, "I put myself in Your hands."

All: Jesus, help us to always love God.

✝ I will be kind to my mother.

✝ I will be kind to someone sick.

✝ I will help feed the poor.

24 Easter

Our Life

Have you ever heard some really good news?
What was it?

Sharing Life

After Jesus died, His friends were very sad.
Then they heard the most wonderful news!
Do you know what it was?
How do you think they felt?

Our Faith

An Easter Play

Narrator: Mary Magdalene was crying outside of Jesus' tomb. Jesus' body was not there. There was a man by the tomb.

Angel: Lady, why are you crying?

Mary: They have taken Jesus away. I do not know where they have put Him.

Narrator: When Mary said this, she saw Jesus standing by her, but she did not know that it was Jesus.

Jesus: Why are you crying? Who are you looking for?

Narrator: Mary thought that Jesus was the gardener.

Mary: If you took Jesus away, tell me where you have put Him. I will go and get Him.

Jesus: Mary!

Mary: Jesus!

Jesus: Go tell My friends that I have risen from the dead.

Narrator: Mary went back to Jesus' friends and told them Jesus was alive!

Coming to Faith

What is your favorite part of the Easter story?
Act out the Easter story with your class.

Practicing Faith

Decorate this banner.

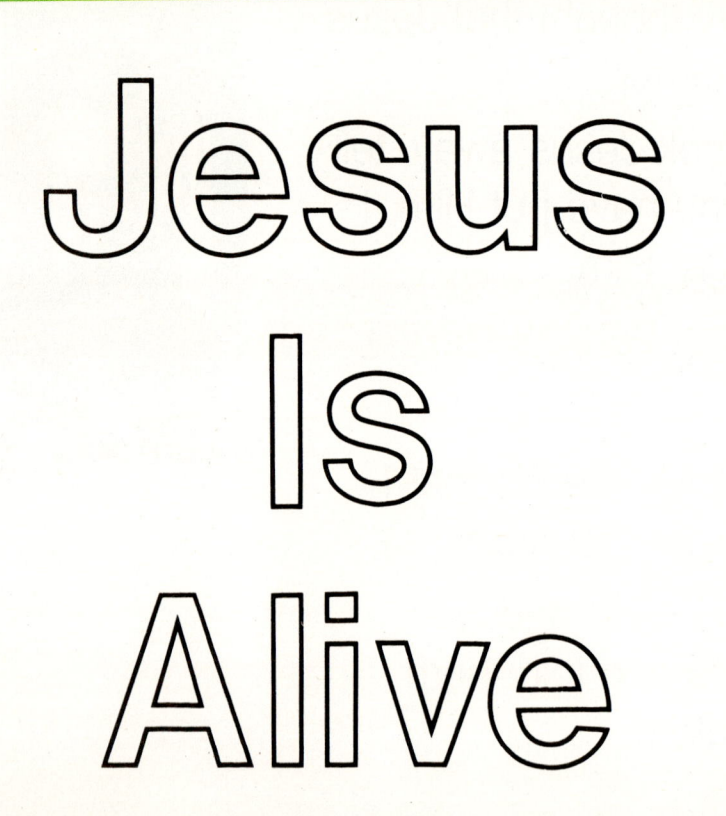

Jesus Is Alive

Tell a friend what the banner means.

✝ Easter Prayer Service

All: Jesus is alive!

Reader: (Read John 20:14–17, text page 103.)

Leader: Jesus gives us new life.

All: Jesus is alive!

Leader: We receive new life at Baptism.

All: Jesus is alive!

Leader: We celebrate Jesus' new life each Sunday.

All: Jesus is alive!

Leader: Jesus is alive! Let us celebrate!

Faith Alive at Home

If possible, take a few minutes during Holy Week to talk about Jesus' Last Supper, His death, and His Resurrection. Use text page 110–113 to do this.

25 Unit III Review

Jesus sends the Holy Spirit.

God the Holy Spirit helped the friends of Jesus to pray and to remember that Jesus wanted them to love others. The Holy Spirit helped them to be fair and to be peacemakers.

The Church begins.

The Church is Jesus Christ and His baptized friends joined together by the Holy Spirit. The Holy Spirit helps the friends of Jesus to be His Church.

We celebrate Baptism.

When we are baptized, we become God's own children. We receive God's own life and love. We become part of the Church.

We celebrate Mass.

Mass is our great celebration together. We listen to God's Word from the Bible. We do what Jesus did at the Last Supper. We receive the Body and Blood of Jesus in Holy Communion.

Unit III Test

Read to me

Fill in the circle beside the correct answer.

1. We belong to Jesus' ____ .
   ○ room   ○ Church   ○ help

2. The ____ is with us today.
   ○ friend   ○ Holy Spirit   ○ children

3. We receive ____ in Holy Communion.
   ○ Jesus   ○ water   ○ cookies

4. In Baptism I became a ____ of God.
   ○ child   ○ flower   ○ dog

5. Draw a picture of yourself loving someone as Jesus did.

189

26 Our Parish Church

Our Life

Read to me

Down in the valley,
In the bottom of the sea,
Lived a crab named Charlie,
Who was cranky as can be.
He was mean and green,
Always ready for a fight.
It's no wonder he was lonely
Every morning, every night.

Down in the valley,
In the bottom of the sea,
Lived a fish named Sharkey,
Who was friendly as can be.
He was kind and good,
Always helpful to a friend,
And he wanted more than anything
To see this sadness end.

So Sharkey got the starfish
And some other fishy friends
To help him send a message
To say, "Our love to you we send.
So, Charlie, when you're lonely,
And need a friend to care,
Come join us at our special place.
You're always welcome there!"

Well, Charlie Crab was happy then;
A smile came to his face.
For now he knew he had good friends
And a special meeting place.

Our parish church is a special place.

What made Charlie the crab happy?
How do you make your friends happy?
How do your friends make you happy when you are sad?
How do you cheer up your friends when they are sad?

Sharing Life

Where is your favorite place to

play   eat   be quiet   talk

Why are they your favorite places?

Do friends need a place to be together? Why?
Do Jesus' friends need a special place to be together? Why?

You Can Learn

- Our parish is a special place.
- Everyone helps in our parish.
- We belong to the Catholic Church.

191

Our Faith

Do friends need a special place to be together? Why?
Where do Jesus' friends gather together?

Our Parish

Our parish is our special place in the Catholic Church. We come together with other Catholic families who live near us.

Our parish belongs to all of us. We learn about Jesus in our parish.
We learn to live as Jesus' friends.

We try to love one another.
We try to be fair to everyone.
We try to be peacemakers.

Everyone is important in our parish family. When visitors come, we say "Welcome to our parish!"

Faith Word
The **parish** is our special place in the Catholic Church.

Each parish has a building called a parish church.

There are so many things that happen in our parish church.
We are baptized there.
We celebrate the Mass there.
We pray and worship there.

Write the name of your parish.
_____
_____

What is a parish?
Do you feel welcome in your parish? Why?

Our Faith (continued)

What is the name of your parish? What do you like to do in your parish?

Helping in Our Parish

Many people make up our parish family.

There are young people and old people, families, and friends.
We all have something special to do.
We are all important in our parish family.

Some people help us to celebrate the Mass.

Some of them read God's word to us.
Some of them give us Holy Communion.

Some people in our parish visit the sick and the lonely.

Some people teach us about God.
Some people help the poor.
Some people work for peace.

The priest in our parish brings us all together.
He leads us as we worship God at Mass.
He helps us to care for one another.

◀ **Write**

the name of your pastor. Call him by name when you meet him.

_____

- -

_____

- -

_____

Who helps in your parish?
What will you do in your parish?

195

Our Faith (continued)

How do the people in your parish help one another? Are you happy to belong to your parish? Why or why not?

Belonging to the Catholic Church

There are thousands and thousands of Catholic parishes like ours all over the world.

The Catholic Church is our special part of the Christian family.

Those who belong to our Church family are called Catholics.

In the Catholic Church, our parishes are grouped together. They make up a diocese.
A diocese has many parishes. The bishop is the leader of our diocese.

The Pope is the leader of the Catholic Church all over the world. The Pope leads and serves us.

Coming to Faith

Many people in our parish do special things. They help one another.

Finish this card.

My name is _____.

I belong to _____ parish.

My pastor is _____.

Someone else who helps in our parish is _____.

Faith Summary

- Our parish is our special place in the Catholic Church.
- Everyone helps in our parish.
- The Pope leads and serves the Catholic Church.

Practicing Faith

Tell three ways people help one another in your parish.

Name one way you would like to help in your parish this week.

Invite one of your friends to visit your parish church.
Write the invitation.

Faith Alive at Home

Reading the *Faith Summary* on page 197 will help your family to learn what was taught this week. Here are some things you may do to help your children know and live their faith.

Talk about the parish
You might like to tell your child about the people in your parish who help. They are those who visit the sick, read the word of God at Mass, give out Holy Communion, serve at the altar, and so on. If possible, introduce your child to one of these ministers and encourage your child to talk to the minister about his or her work.

Review Test

Circle the correct word.

1. My ____ is a very special place.

   parish   car

2. Our parish has a special building called the parish ____.

   house   church

3. We give ____ to God in our parish.

   praise   name

4. The ____ is the leader of the Catholic Church.

   people   Pope

5. Circle how you feel about belonging to your parish.

   ☺   ☹

Pray for the Church
Encourage your child to pray for your parish and the Church throughout the world. Here is a prayer you might use.

† Jesus, bless
our parish family.
Bless Your Church
all over the world.
Help us to live like You.
Help us to share Your
Good News with everyone.

27 Our Catholic Church

Our Life

What do you see in these pictures?
Do any of these things help you think about God?
What else helps you think about God?

When do you think about God?

We pray to God.

Sharing Life

Why do these things help you think about God?
What do you want to say to God?
Say it in your heart or tell it to a friend.

You Can Learn

- Catholics pray to God.
- Catholics celebrate the sacraments.
- Our Catholic Church helps us to be holy.

Our Faith

Do you pray to God? How? When do you pray?

Catholics Pray

All around the world, Catholics pray to God.

We tell God how wonderful God is.
We tell God we are sorry.
We ask God to help us.
We thank God for all God's gifts.

There are prayers we say together and prayers we say alone.

Sometimes we pray in our own words.
We talk to God as a friend.
Sometimes we sing our prayers.

Sometimes we pray the prayer that Jesus taught us, the Our Father.
The Our Father is a prayer that all Christians pray.

Catholics pray to Mary, the Mother of Jesus.
We ask Mary to pray to God for us.

Here is a beautiful prayer to Mary that Catholics pray. It is called the Hail Mary.

◀ **Decorate and Learn** this prayer to Mary.

† Hail Mary, full of grace,
the Lord is with you;
blessed are you among women,
and blessed is the fruit
of your womb, Jesus.
Holy Mary, Mother of God,
pray for us sinners
now and at the hour of our death.
Amen.

Why do Catholics pray to Mary?
When will you pray the Hail Mary?

Our Faith (continued)

What is your favorite prayer? When do you pray with your whole parish family?

Celebrating the Sacraments

In our Church we worship God. We celebrate the sacraments.

The sacraments help us to know that God is with us.

In the sacraments, our Church does what Jesus did for His friends.

Jesus welcomed all people into His community of friends.

In the sacrament of Baptism, our Church welcomes all people into our Church community.

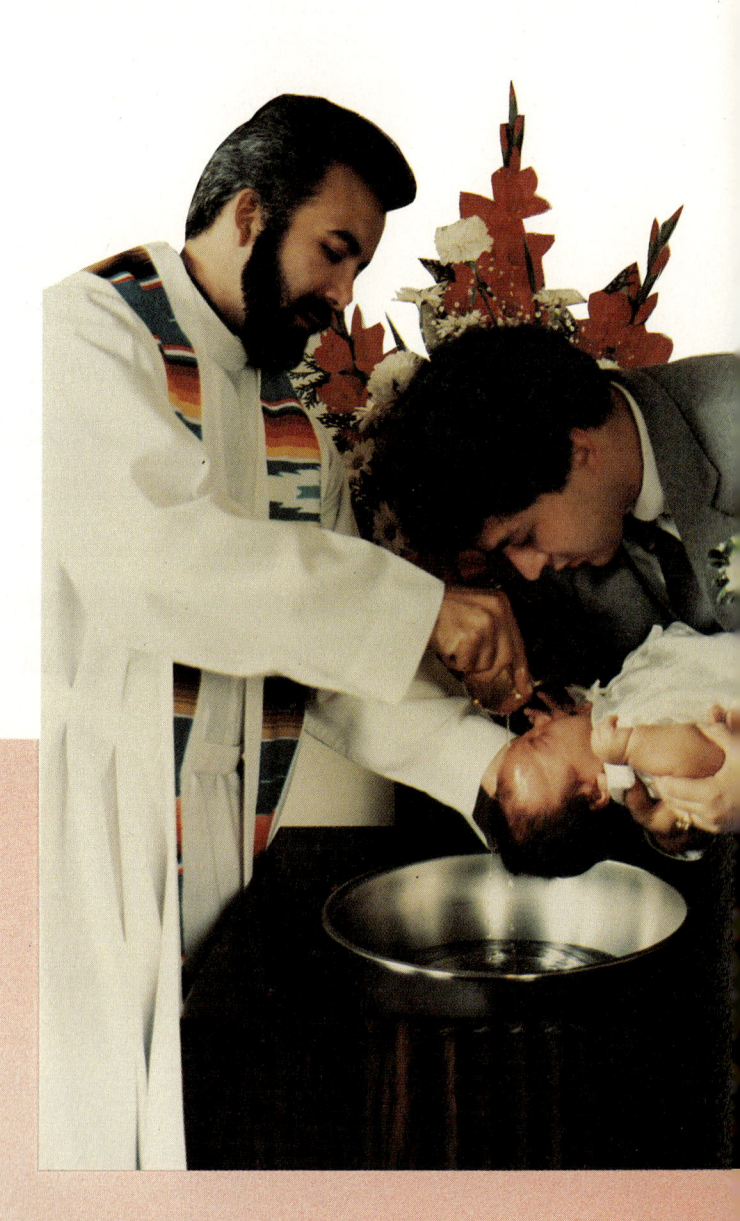

Faith Word
To **worship** is to give honor to God.

Jesus forgave people.
In the sacrament of Reconciliation, the Church brings us God's forgiveness.

Jesus fed people who were hungry.
In the sacrament of the Eucharist, the Church gives us Jesus Himself to be our food in Holy Communion.

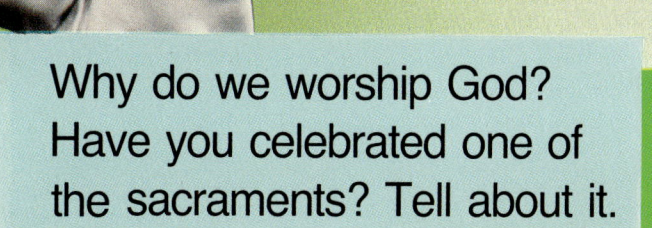

Why do we worship God? Have you celebrated one of the sacraments? Tell about it.

205

Our Faith (continued)

What sacraments can you name?
How does Jesus want His
friends to live?

Being Holy

We are Jesus' friends, the Church.
We are holy people.
To be holy means to belong to God
and to live as Jesus taught us.
Our Church helps us to be holy.

This is how we become holy.

   We talk to God.
   We talk to others about God.
   We live as friends of Jesus.

The Bible tells us, "You are called
to be a holy people. You belong to
God. You are God's people."

From 1 Peter 2:9–10

Coming to Faith

Circle the word that goes in the space.

1. Catholics ask God for help. Catholics ____ to God.

   holy   pray   worships

2. Our Church helps us to remember we belong to God. We are to be ____.

   holy   pray   worships

Tell what you like best about being a Catholic.

Faith Summary

- Catholics pray every day.
- Catholics celebrate the sacraments.
- To be holy means to belong to God.

Practicing Faith

Circle how you will pray this week.

I will say my morning prayers.

I will say prayers before meals.

I will pray for our Holy Father, the Pope.

I will pray for all people.

I will sing to God.

I will give honor to God.

I will thank God for all God's gifts.

I will let everyone know I belong to God.

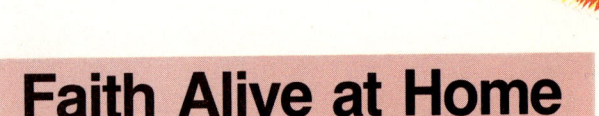

Faith Alive at Home

Reading the *Faith Summary* on page 207 will help your family to learn what was taught this week. Here are some things you may do to help your children know and live their faith.

Ways to pray
Your child has circled ways that he or she will pray this week. Help him or her to remember to do them. Choose one that you can do together.

Review Test

Circle the correct word.

1. _____ pray every day.

    Catholics   Animals

2. Catholics help one another to be _____.

    sad   holy

3. We are holy _____.

    animals   people

4. Catholics celebrate the _____.

    sacraments   candles

5. What is your favorite prayer? When will you pray this prayer?

† **Reflective prayer**
Before your child goes to bed, you may want to review reflectively with him or her how God was real to him or her that day. You might start by asking, "Did you help anyone today? Did you play fairly? Did you do your best work in school?" Then explain that each time he or she did one of these things, God was with him or her. After the reflection, thank God for God's presence.

28 The Church Helps People

Our Life

Read to me

One Saturday, Ann and Danny were alone eating a delicious supper of fried chicken. The telephone rang. Ann got very excited. "That must be Laurie," Ann said as she dropped her chicken leg and ran to answer the phone.

Then it happened! Danny had eaten all his chicken. But Ann's chicken leg was just sitting there on her plate begging him to eat it. In his head he could hear it saying, "Eat me! Eat me!"

Danny knew it wasn't fair to eat Ann's chicken. But before he knew it his fingers had walked across the table, grabbed the chicken leg, and pushed it into his mouth.

Just as Danny was licking the last of the chicken from his fingers, Ann came back.

She stopped suddenly. Her mouth fell open! She shouted, "What happened to my chicken? Danny, I can't believe you are so mean! How could you eat my chicken? I hope Mom keeps you in the house for a month!"

We help other people.

Do you think Danny was fair? Explain.

Have you ever been treated unfairly? How did you feel?

Sharing Life

Have you ever been unfair to anyone?
What did you do?

Why does Jesus want us to be fair to everyone?

You Can Learn

- In our Church, we learn to be fair to others.
- In our Church, we learn to bring peace to others.
- In our Church, we tell the Good News of Jesus to others.

211

Our Faith

What does it mean to be fair? How does God want you to treat other people?

Being Fair

The Bible tells us a story about a man who was not fair.

Read to me from the Bible

Once there was a servant who owed his master a lot of money. He could not pay what he owed. He begged his master to give him more time. The master felt sorry for his servant. He said, "You do not have to pay me back any money."

The servant was very happy. Then that servant went to another man who owed him some money. The man begged, "Please give me a little more time and I will pay you what I owe you!"

The servant said, "No! You must pay now."

The master was very angry at the servant who was not fair.
From Matthew 18:22–34

The first servant was treated fairly. But he was not fair to the man who owed him money.

Jesus shows us how to be fair. Being fair means treating people the way we want them to treat us.

Jesus teaches us that it does not matter how young or old a person is. It does not matter what color skin a person has. God wants us to be fair with everyone.

When we are fair, we show people that God loves everyone.

What does it mean to be fair? Why should we be fair to everyone?

213

Our Faith (continued)

To whom does God want us to be fair?
What would happen if all people were fair to one another?

We Bring Peace to Others

When we are fair to one another, we can live in peace.

Peace is a wonderful thing.
Peace means not fighting.
Peace means not worrying.
Peace means being quiet inside ourselves.

Jesus gives us His gift of peace.
Jesus said,
"My peace is My gift to you."

From John 14:27

In the Church we try to live in peace with one another. Jesus wants us to be peacemakers.

Jesus said,
"Happy are the peacemakers. They will be called the children of God."

From Matthew 5:9

◀ **Draw or paste** a picture of someone being a peacemaker.

How can you be a peacemaker? When will you do it?

Our Faith (continued)

Who helps you to make peace?
Who helps you to love others?

We Tell the Good News

Jesus tells us the Good News that God loves us all.
In the Church we tell the Good News to others.

In our world, there are happy people and sad people.
Some people have enough food and some do not.

Some people have families to love them and some people are alone.
They need to know God loves them.

They will know God loves them when we love and help them.

Coming to Faith

What does it mean to be fair?
What is a peacemaker?

Check the things you feel peaceful about. Then check the things you worry about.

I feel peaceful about
- [ ] school.
- [ ] my family.
- [ ] the way I look.

I worry about
- [ ] school.
- [ ] my family.
- [ ] the way I look.

Look at one thing you checked, "I feel peaceful about."
Tell why you are peaceful.

Look at one thing you checked, "I worry about."
Tell someone about it. Will you ask him or her to help you?

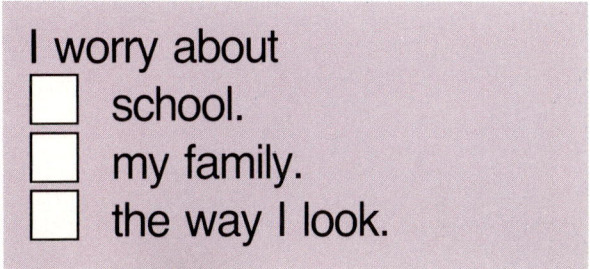

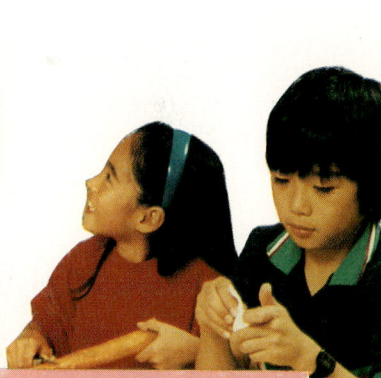

Faith Summary

- Catholics try to treat others fairly.
- Catholics try to live in peace.
- Catholics bring the Good News of God's love to others.

217

Practicing Faith

To whom will you be fair?
Draw what you will do.

When will you try to be a peacemaker?
How will you go about it?

Faith Alive at Home

Reading the *Faith Summary* on page 217 will help your family to learn what was taught this week. Here are some things you may do to help your children know and live their faith.

Sharing worries
In *Coming to Faith* your child checked some things she or he feels peaceful about or worries about. Go over the list with him or her. Take some time to talk about your child's worries.

Review Test

Circle the correct word.

1. Jesus gave the gift of ____ to us.

    peace   sadness

2. I should always play ____.

    unfairly   fairly

3. Catholics bring the ____ News to others.

    Bad   Good

4. Jesus said, "Happy are the ____."

    peacemakers   troublemakers

5. I will try to be fair ____.

    sometimes   always

Talk about fairness
Help your child in his or her daily life to notice opportunities for practicing fairness with others.

† Quiet time
Spend some quiet, reflective time praying with your child about his or her worries. Encourage your child to place his or her worries in Jesus' hands and to ask Jesus to help him or her not to worry.

29 God Forgives Us

Our Life

Read to me

The torn and tattered teddy bear sat forlornly by the door. Meg and Ed saw it. "Look, there's Mikey's teddy bear," Ed said. "Let's play catch with it."

Meg grabbed the teddy bear and tossed it up in the air. As Ed caught the teddy bear, its leg fell off and the stuffing fell out.

"Let's throw it in the trash can and get out of here fast!" cried Meg.

That night Meg and Ed could hear Mikey sobbing. He could not sleep without his arm around his teddy bear.

Mom asked Ed and Meg, "Have you seen Mikey's teddy bear? I've looked everywhere, but I can't find it. Mikey is crying for it."

Meg and Ed looked at each other. They ran out to the trash can. Meg shook the dirt off the teddy bear and ran back with it.

Mikey was sitting on Mom's lap. Meg said, "Mikey, we're sorry. We were just having fun."

Ed said, "Please don't cry, Mikey. We didn't mean to throw it away. We were just scared. We'll mend your teddy bear's leg."

God always forgives us.

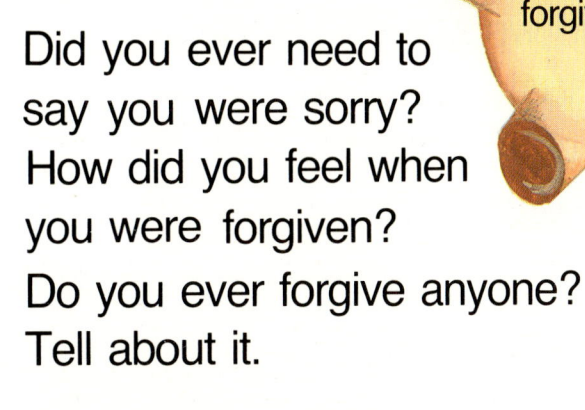

Did you ever need to say you were sorry?
How did you feel when you were forgiven?
Do you ever forgive anyone? Tell about it.

Sharing Life

What does it mean to forgive someone?
Why do we sometimes need to ask God to forgive us?
Do you believe God forgives us? Why?

You Can Learn
- Sometimes we need to say we are sorry.
- Jesus brings us God's forgiveness.
- The Church forgives us in God's name.

Our Faith

Why do we sometimes do things that are wrong? When do we need to say, "I am sorry"?

Being Sorry

We belong to God.
We are baptized.
We are God's children.
We know that God wants us to love God, love others, and love ourselves.

Sometimes people do not live as they should.
They do things they know they should not do.
They do not live as children of God. They sin.

When we do something we should not do, we need to show we are sorry. There are lots of ways to say to others, "I am sorry."

We can do something nice for them.
We can give a hug.
We can shake hands.
We can say what is in our hearts.

◀ **Draw**
a picture that shows how you like to say you are sorry.

How can you show you are sorry?
What do you do to try to make up?

Our Faith (continued)

> Think of a time when you told someone you were sorry. What did the person say or do?

God's Forgiveness

God will always love us, no matter what we do. God always forgives us if we are sorry. In the Bible there is a story about God's love and forgiveness.

Read to me from the Bible

Once there was a young man who decided to take all his money and leave his father's home. For a while he had a lot of fun doing just what he wanted to do. He had new friends. But when all his money was gone, all his new friends left him. He had no place to stay and nothing to eat. He knew he had been wrong. He decided to go back home and tell his father how sorry he was.

His father was so happy to see him, he forgave his foolish son and had a party to welcome him home.

From Luke 15:11–24

Jesus tells us that God will always forgive us, just like the father in the story.

▸ **Use**
the picture to tell the story of the forgiving father.

Will God always forgive us? How do you know?

225

Our Faith (continued)

How do you know when someone forgives you? How do you feel when you are forgiven?

The Church Forgives

In the Catholic Church we have a wonderful way to celebrate that God forgives us. It is called the sacrament of Reconciliation. We pray and thank God for loving us and forgiving us.

We meet with the priest.
We tell God and one another we are sorry for our sins.
The priest forgives us in God's name.
How wonderful it is to know we have been forgiven.

When you are ready, you will be able to celebrate the sacrament of Reconciliation with your parish family.

Coming to Faith

Does God always forgive us if we are sorry? How do you know?

How does the Catholic Church celebrate God's love and forgiveness?

Draw how you feel when you are forgiven.

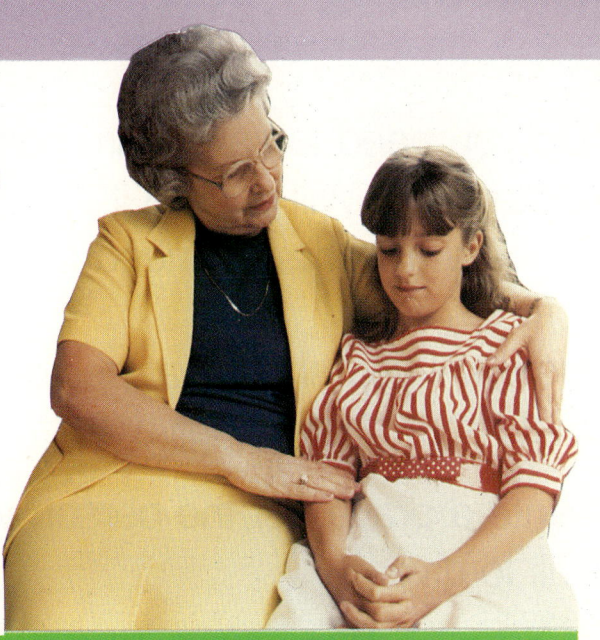

Faith Summary

- Jesus brings us God's forgiveness.
- God always forgives us if we are sorry.
- The Church forgives in God's name.

Practicing Faith

Do you need to say, "I am sorry," to anyone? Will you do it?
Is there anyone you need to forgive?
How will you show that person that he or she is forgiven?

Write a prayer for the person you will forgive.

> Dear God,
>
> I forgive _____
>
> for _____
>
> because _____

Will you always ask God to forgive you?

Review Test

Circle the correct word.

1. God forgives us if we say we are ____ .

    sorry   happy

2. ____ brings us God's forgiveness.

    John   Jesus

3. We are God's ____ .

    flowers   children

4. How do you feel when you have been forgiven?

    happy   sad

Faith Alive at Home

Reading the *Faith Summary* on page 227 will help your family to learn what was taught this week. Here are some things you may do to help your children know and live their faith.

Draw a picture
You might want to remind your child that God always forgives us if we are sorry. Encourage your child to draw a picture of himself or herself saying, "I am sorry!"

Sharing prayers
Ask your child to share his or her prayer of forgiveness with you.
Go over this part of the Our Father with your child:
† "Forgive us our trespasses as we forgive those who trespass against us."
Point out the importance of forgiving others if we wish to be forgiven ourselves.

30 God's Life Lasts Forever

Our Life

Imagine you are in second grade.
Ask yourself these questions.

Will I look the same as I do today?
Will I be as tall?
Will I have the same number of teeth?
Will I be in the same classroom?
Will I have the same teacher?

We will be happy with God forever.

Sharing Life

What do you think will stay the same about you? Why?

What do you think will be different? Why?

Does anything stay the same forever?

What do you think lasts forever?

You Can Learn

- Jesus wants us to be with Him forever.
- God's love for us will never end.
- Jesus will be with us during the summer.

231

Our Faith

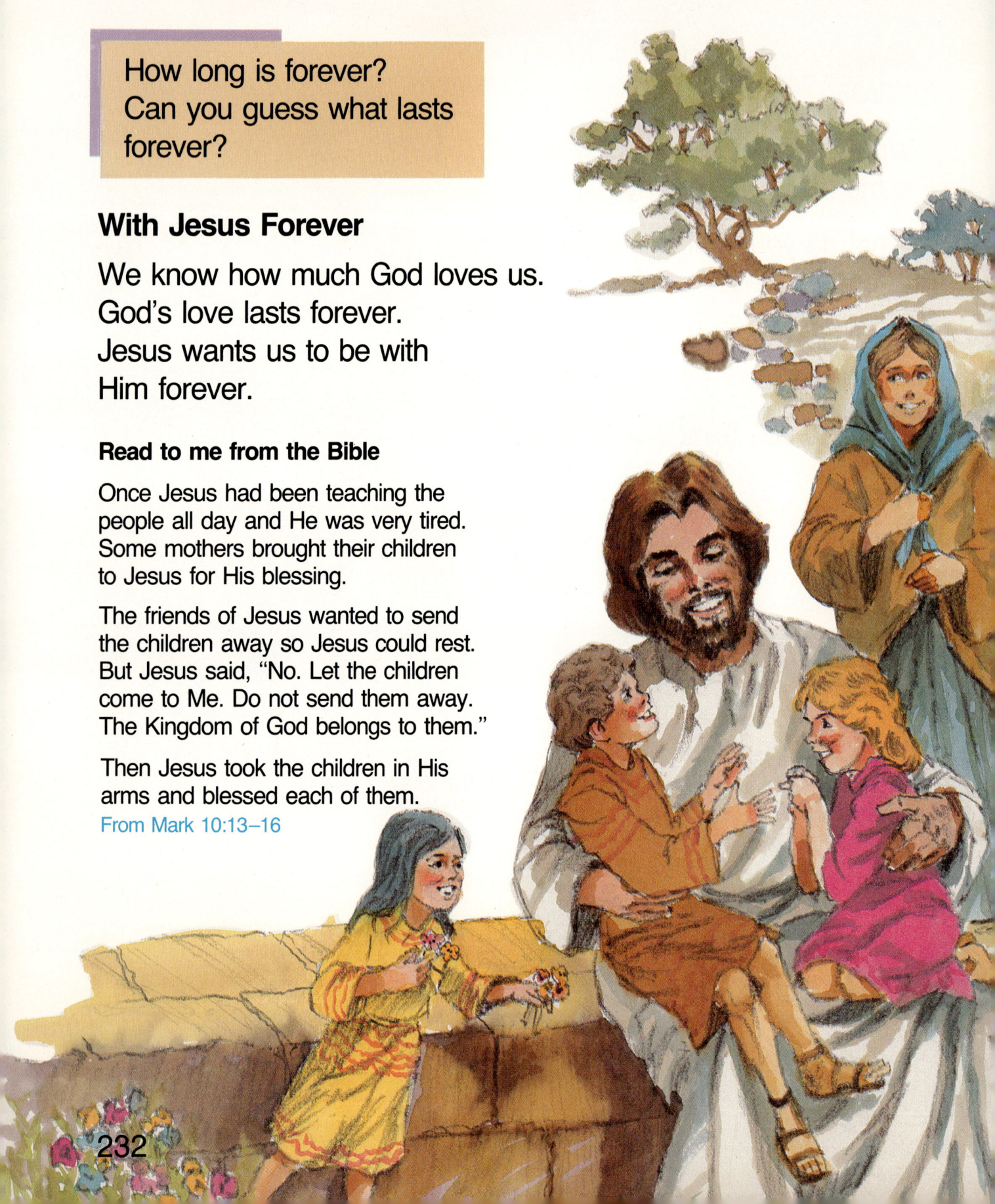

How long is forever?
Can you guess what lasts forever?

With Jesus Forever

We know how much God loves us.
God's love lasts forever.
Jesus wants us to be with
Him forever.

Read to me from the Bible

Once Jesus had been teaching the people all day and He was very tired. Some mothers brought their children to Jesus for His blessing.

The friends of Jesus wanted to send the children away so Jesus could rest. But Jesus said, "No. Let the children come to Me. Do not send them away. The Kingdom of God belongs to them."

Then Jesus took the children in His arms and blessed each of them.

From Mark 10:13–16

If we live as children of God, we will be happy with God forever in heaven.
Jesus will be with us forever.

What did Jesus tell us would last forever?
How would you feel if Jesus put His arms around you and blessed you?

Our Faith (continued)

Tell the story of Jesus and the children.
What Good News does the story tell?
Do you believe it? Why?

God's Love Lasts Forever

We have learned many things about God. We call these wonderful things Good News.

Here is the Good News we have learned this year.
- God made our world.
- God made us and loves us.
- God gave us God's Son, Jesus.
- We try to follow Jesus.
- Jesus showed us how to love God, one another, and ourselves.
- Jesus taught us how to be fair and live in peace.

We can live forever in heaven with God.

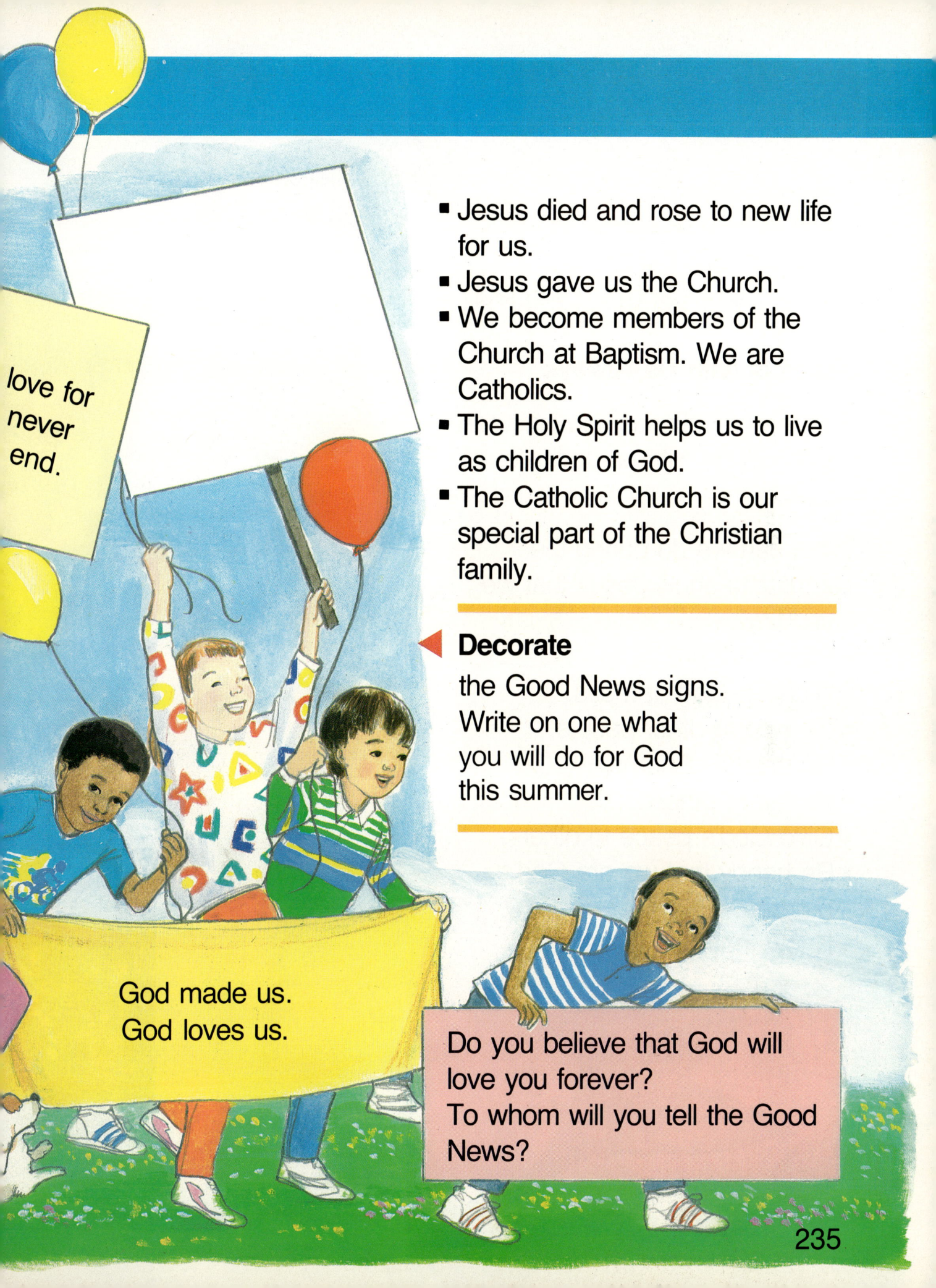

- Jesus died and rose to new life for us.
- Jesus gave us the Church.
- We become members of the Church at Baptism. We are Catholics.
- The Holy Spirit helps us to live as children of God.
- The Catholic Church is our special part of the Christian family.

Decorate

the Good News signs. Write on one what you will do for God this summer.

love for never end.

God made us.
God loves us.

Do you believe that God will love you forever?
To whom will you tell the Good News?

Our Faith (continued)

Do you know something that lasts forever? What is it? How does that make you feel?

Jesus Is with Us Always

Summer vacation is coming soon. Jesus will be with us during our vacation.

What can we do during the summer to show Jesus that we love Him?
- Pray.
- Worship God at Mass.
- Be kind to other people.
- Be helpful at home.
- Be fair to others.
- Give God's peace to others.
- Be happy that we are God's children.
- Know that God loves us.

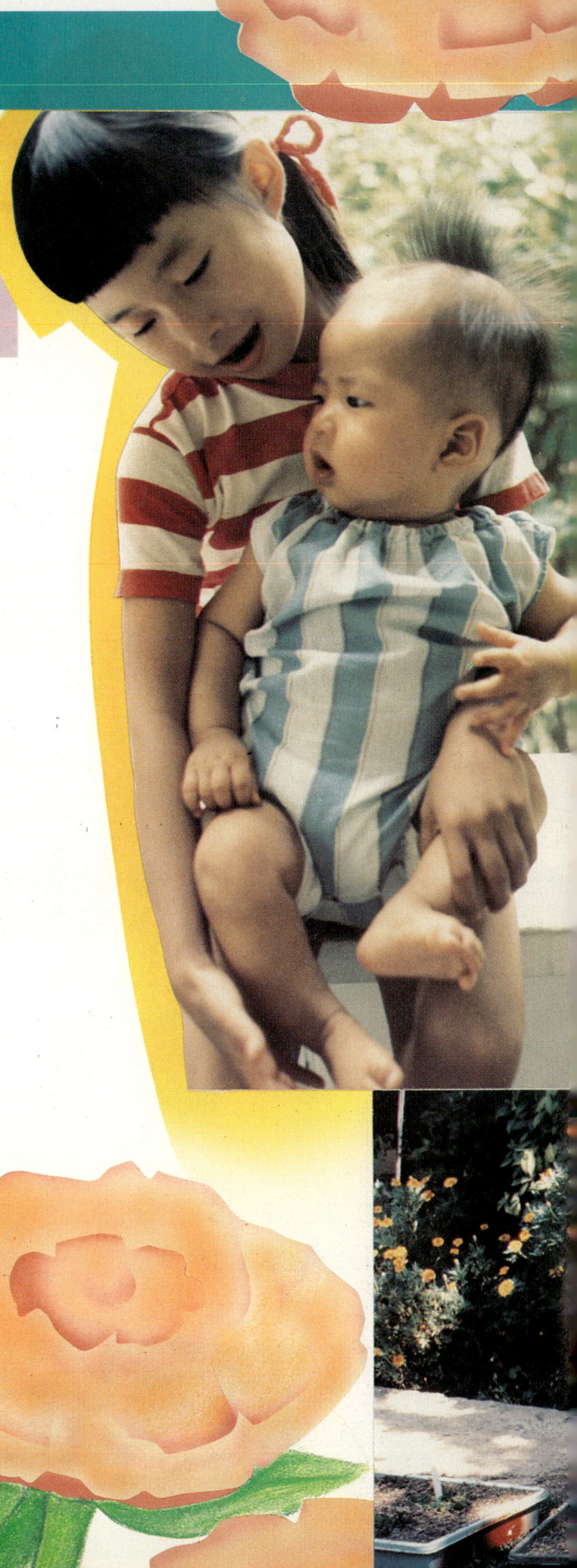

Coming to Faith

Do you believe that you can live forever with God? Why?

Draw and tell about one thing you learned about God this year. The pictures in this book will help you.

What I Learned About God.

Faith Summary

- Jesus wants us to be with Him forever.
- God's love will never end.
- Jesus will be with us during the summer.

Practicing Faith

My Summer Plan for God
Summer vacation is here. We want to remember all that we learned.

How will you remember that God is with you during your vacation?

Circle what you will do this summer to show that you are God's child.

- I will pray.
- I will worship God at Mass.
- I will be kind to others.
- I will be helpful at home.
- I will give God's peace to others.
- I will be fair to others.

Faith Alive at Home

Reading the *Faith Summary* on page 237 will help your family to learn what was taught this week. Here are some things you may do to help your children know and live their faith.

Remembering Baptism
You may want to discuss with your child God's unending love. Here is a passage from the Baptism ceremony to pray with your child. Lighting a candle, you pray:

† "Receive the light of Jesus. Keep this light burning brightly.
Walk as children of the light.
We will all be together
with God forever and ever."

Then recall for your child some of the most important truths he or she learned this year. Discuss with your child the importance of God's word and presence in his or her life. You may wish to end by saying this prayer together:

Review Test

Circle the correct word.

1. God will stay with me ____.

    a day   forever

2. God's ____ will last forever.

    love   fear

3. Jesus blessed the ____.

    day   children

4. Draw one thing you will do this summer to show you are God's child.

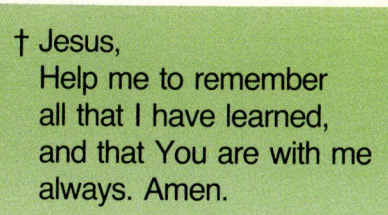

† Jesus,
Help me to remember all that I have learned, and that You are with me always. Amen.

239

31 A Prayer Service for Forgiveness

Opening Prayer: Jesus, You told us in the story of the Forgiving Father that God always loves us and forgives us. Sometimes we need to come to You and say we are sorry. Help us to remember that You will always love and forgive us.

Reader: Once there was a young man who decided to take all his money and leave his father's home. For a while he had a lot of fun doing just what he wanted to do. When all his money was gone, all his new friends left him. He had no place to stay and nothing to eat. He knew he had been wrong. He decided to go back home and tell his father how sorry he was.

Leader: Now we will say "We are sorry." We will ask Jesus to forgive us. We will forgive one another.

Child 1: For the times that we fought with a brother, a sister, or a friend, we say

All: Jesus, we are sorry.

Child 2: For the times we took something from our friends, we say

All: Jesus, we are sorry.

Child 3: For the times we disobeyed our parents and did not show respect to old people, we say

All: Jesus, we are sorry.

Leader: We have all said we are sorry. Let us offer each other the sign of peace.

Conclude by playing quiet music.

32 Unit IV Review

We belong to a parish.

In our parish we come together to learn about Jesus and how to live as Jesus' friends. Everyone is welcome in our parish family.

We belong to the Catholic Church.

Our Church helps us to be holy people. We celebrate the sacraments. In the sacraments our Church does what Jesus did for His friends.

We learn how to live in our Church.

In our Church we learn how to be fair to others. Being fair means treating people the way we want them to treat us. When we are fair to one another, we can live in peace.

The Church brings God's forgiveness.

In the Catholic Church we have a wonderful way to celebrate that God forgives us. It is called the sacrament of Reconciliation. We pray and thank God for loving us and forgiving us.

God's life lasts forever.

If we live as children of God, we will be happy with God forever in heaven.

Unit IV Test

Read to me

Circle the correct word.

1. In our parish everyone is ____.
   hurt   welcome

2. Our Church helps us to be ____ people.
   holy   sad

3. When we are fair, we can live in ____.
   hate   peace

4. The sacrament of Reconciliation celebrates God's ____.
   forgiveness   anger

5. Draw a picture that shows how you will be with Jesus this summer.

33 Second Semester Review

Jesus Christ sends the Holy Spirit.

The Holy Spirit helps the friends of Jesus. The Holy Spirit helps them to be peacemakers.

The Holy Spirit comes to us when we are baptized.

When we are baptized, we become part of the Church.

We receive God's own life and love.

We belong to the Catholic Church.

Everyone is welcome in our Church. The Church helps us to be holy people.

We celebrate the sacraments and try to live fairly and to be peacemakers.

If we live as children of God, we will be happy with God forever in heaven.

Second Semester Test

Read to me

Fill in the circle next to each correct answer.

1. The Holy Spirit helps ___.
   ○ me   ○ animals   ○ plants

2. We are part of the ___.
   ○ circus   ○ sea   ○ Church

3. The celebration of Jesus' Last Supper is called ___.
   ○ Good Friday ○ Christmas   ○ Mass

4. The ___ is the Good News of Jesus.
   ○ singing   ○ Gospel   ○ loving

5. Jesus' Church is for ___.
   ○ no one   ○ someone   ○ everyone

6. Draw a picture of one way you will be fair to someone.

Glossary

Baptism
The sacrament that gives us a share in God's life and makes us God's own children and members of Jesus' Church.

Bible
The book of God's Word.

Blessed Trinity
The three Persons in one God: the Father, the Son, and the Holy Spirit.

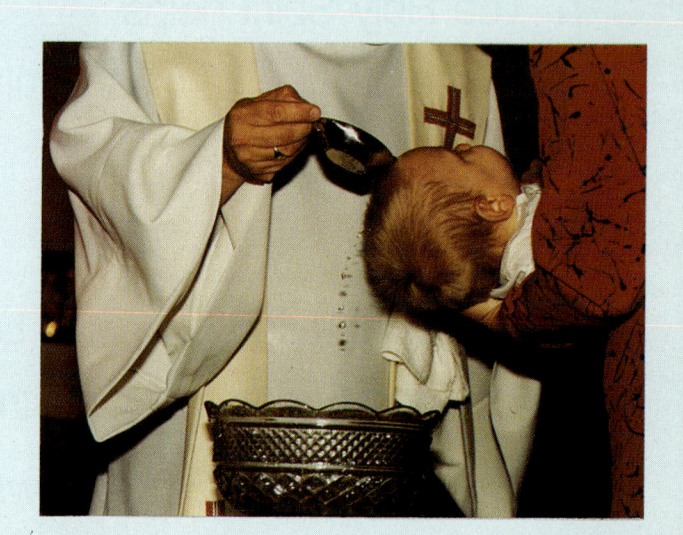

Catholic Church
The baptized followers of Jesus who are joined together by the Holy Spirit under the leadership of the Pope and bishops.

Christians
The followers of Jesus Christ.

Creation
Everything made by God.

Easter Sunday
The day Jesus rose from the dead.

Eucharist
The sacrament in which we receive the Body and Blood of Jesus Christ.

Good Friday
The day Jesus died for all His friends.

Gospel
The Good News that God loves us and gives us Jesus Christ, God's Son.

Grace
God's own life and love in us.

Holy Spirit
The third Person of the Blessed Trinity, the Helper sent to the Church.

Jesus Christ
The Son of God and the Son of Mary, the second Person of the Blessed Trinity.

Last Supper
The last meal Jesus had with His friends before He died.

Mass
The special celebration in which we hear God's Word and share the Body and Blood of Jesus.

Parish church
The special place where Jesus' friends come together.

Prayer
Talking and listening to God.

Sin
The act of freely choosing to do what we know to be wrong. We disobey God's Law on purpose.

The Mass ends.

The priest blesses us and says, "Go in peace to love and serve the Lord."

We answer,

"Thanks be to God."

16   Cut on this line

My Mass Book Grade 1

God gives the gift of Holy Communion.

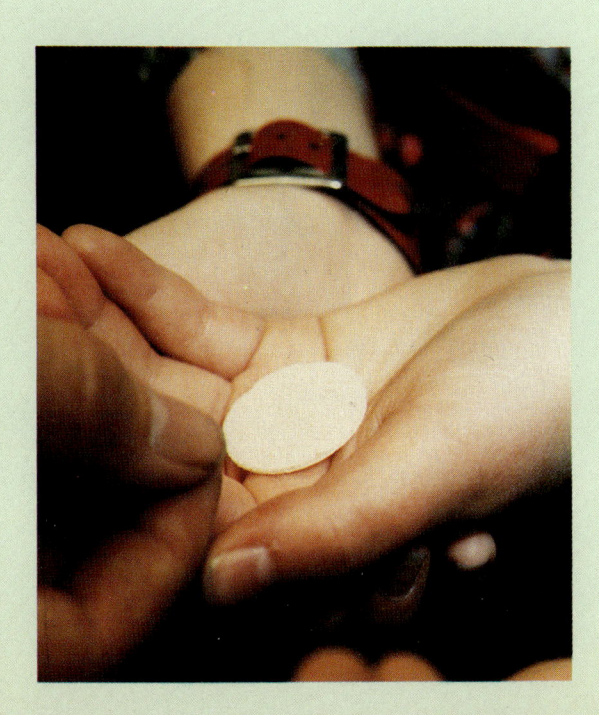

We ask God to forgive us.

"Lord, have mercy,
Christ, have mercy,
Lord, have mercy."

249

The Mass begins.

We stand and pray.

"✝ In the name of the Father,
and of the Son,
and of the Holy Spirit."

Cut on this line

Liturgy of the Word

We listen to God's Word.
The reader says,
"This is the word of the Lord."

We answer,
"Thanks be to God."

250

At Communion time you can pray, too.

You can say,

"Jesus,
    come and live
        in my heart."

We share the gift of peace.

We say,
"Peace be with you."

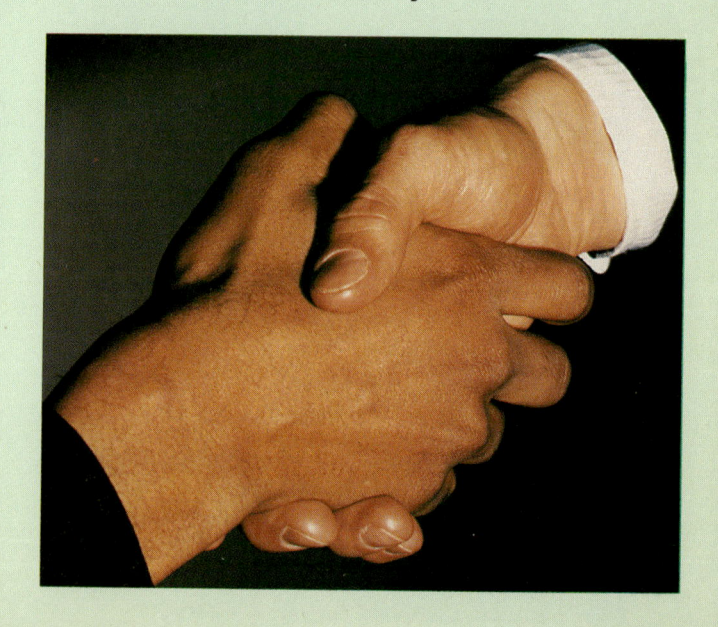

Fold on this line

We pray the prayer that Jesus taught us.

"Our Father, who art in heaven,
hallowed be thy name;
thy kingdom come;
thy will be done on earth
as it is in heaven.
Give us this day our daily bread;
and forgive us our trespasses
as we forgive those
who trespass against us;
and lead us not into temptation,
but deliver us from evil."

We stand for the Gospel.

The priest or deacon says,
"The Lord be with you."

We answer,

"And also with you."

After the gospel, the priest or deacon says,

"This is the gospel of the Lord."

We say,

"Praise to You, Lord Jesus Christ."

The priest says and does what Jesus did at the Last Supper.

"This is my body which will be given up for you."

Liturgy of the Eucharist

The priest invites us to pray,
"Lift up your hearts."

We answer,

"We lift them up to the Lord."

Our gifts of bread and wine are carried to the altar.

The priest prepares our gifts to be offered to God.

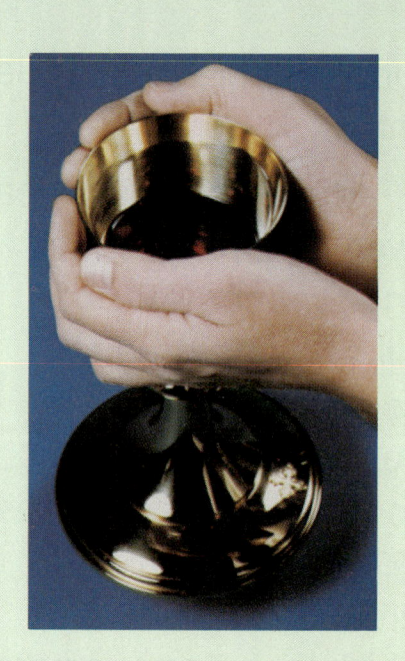

6

"This is the cup of my blood."

11

Cut on this line

We pray,
"Holy,
　　Holy,
　　　　Holy,
Lord, God of power and might; . . ."

We remember what Jesus said and did at the Last Supper.

Fold on this line

252

8

9

I believe in God,

the Father almighty,

Creator of heaven and earth.

The rest of the Apostles' Creed will be taught in Grades 2 and 3.

Cut on this line

Prayers and Practices for Grade 1

Hail Mary

Hail Mary, full of grace!
the Lord is with you;
blessed are you among women,
blessed is the fruit
of your womb, Jesus.
Holy Mary, Mother of God,
pray for us sinners
now and at the hour of our death.
Amen.

Fold on this line

Sign of the Cross

In the name of the Father,
and of the Son,
and of the Holy Spirit.
Amen.

Glory to the Father

Glory to the Father,
and to the Son,
and to the Holy Spirit.
As it was in the beginning,
is now, and will be forever.
Amen.

253

My name is
_____
_____.

My parish is
_____
_____.

Catholic Practices for Grade 1

You bless yourself with the Sign of the Cross.

You make the Sign of the Cross with your right hand.

You use holy water as a sign of your Baptism.

You pray before and after meals.

You pray when you awake and before you go to sleep.

You go to Mass on Sunday or Saturday evening.

You genuflect on your right knee as you enter your pew in church.

Morning Offering

My God, I offer You today
All that I think and do and say,
Uniting it with what was done
On earth, by Jesus Christ,
Your Son.

Grace Before Meals

Bless us, O Lord,
and these Your gifts,
which we are about to receive
from Your bounty,
through Christ our Lord. Amen.

Our Father

Our Father, who art in heaven,
hallowed be Thy name;
Thy kingdom come;
Thy will be done on earth
as it is in heaven.
Give us this day our daily bread;
and forgive us our trespasses
as we forgive those
who trespass against us;
and lead us not into temptation
but deliver us from evil.
Amen.

Let us ask the saints to help us live as friends of Jesus.

Saint Vincent de Paul,
    pray for us.
Saint Thérèse,
    pray for us.
Saint Nicholas,
    pray for us.

May all the saints in heaven pray for us.
May they help us to always live as friends of Jesus.
Amen.

My Saints Book

Saint Nicholas

Everyone loved good Saint Nicholas. He was a holy priest and a good bishop. When people were in trouble, he was always there to help them. Nicholas had a special love for the poor. He helped them without letting others know about it. He loved children in a special way, too. He did many kind, loving things for them. We celebrate the feast of Saint Nicholas on December 6.

Draw a picture

of something you can do to help the poor.

Saint Vincent de Paul

Saint Vincent de Paul was a holy priest. He was captured by pirates. For two years he lived as a slave in Africa. When he was freed, Saint Vincent went back to France. He was a great friend of the poor and the lonely. He tried to help those who were still slaves. Many men and women joined in his work. We celebrate the feast of Saint Vincent de Paul on September 27.

Cut on this line

Saint Thérèse of the Child Jesus

Saint Thérèse was a very happy child. Her parents taught her about Jesus, God's greatest gift to us. Thérèse loved Jesus so much she wanted to give her whole life to Him. She became a Carmelite Sister. Thérèse did many little, loving things for others. She was specially kind to those whom no one else liked. We call her the Little Flower of Jesus. We celebrate her feast day on October 1.

256

Write

the name of someone you know who is in trouble. Tell what you can do to help this person.

Name
_____
_____

I will
_____
_____
_____
_____

Fold on this line

Write

in the flower, one kind thing you can do to show your love for Jesus.